A Practical Guide to

Designing for the Web

by Mark Boulton

A Practical Guide to Designing for the Web
by Mark Boulton

Published in 2009 by Mark Boulton Design Ltd
Studio Two, The Coach House
Stanwell Road
Penarth
CF64 3EU
United Kingdom

On the web: **www.fivesimplesteps.co.uk**
Please send errors to **errata@fivesimplesteps.co.uk**

Publisher: Mark Boulton Design Ltd.
Printer: Qualitech Group, UK
Production Editor: Robert Mills
Interior Design: Mark Boulton, Nick Boulton, Benn Pearson
Cover Design: Nick Boulton

ISBN: 978-0-9561740-1-7

A catalogue record of this book is available from the British Library.

Contents

This little book is about graphic design. It's a book about the craft of graphic design practice as applied to the web. It's not a book about CSS or Usability. I may well touch on those subjects throughout, but only to support a point I'm making in relation to design.

Web design should use the principles of graphic design, but the topic of web design tends to focus on web standards, browser technology, user behaviour and backend development. Many web design books touch on some elements of graphic design, but they usually address the subject briefly and superficially. Even most graphic design books just show pretty pictures of other people's work. There are not enough books outlining the principles, practicalities and tools of the graphic design trade.

Who Should Read This Book?

A Practical Guide to Designing for the Web is for people who want to learn the basics of graphic design and apply them to their web designs–producing more effective, polished, detailed and professional sites. It's also helpful for graphic designers who want to brush up on the basics or learn how to integrate what they already know about design with the demands and quirks of designing specifically for the web.

Some Assumptions

- That although the book contains little HTML or CSS, it assumes that you have a working knowledge of web standards.

- That you work in web design and development. Business owners and managers and others who want a well–designed site may also benefit from reading this book, but the book is directed at the people who plan and create websites.

- That this book doesn't aim to be a definitive guide to web design or graphic design. It simply presents some of the theory, tips and processes I've learnt in the past fifteen years.

Credit

I never imagined I'd ever finish writing this book. Without the help of the following people, it simply would not have been possible:

Carolyn Wood, whose enduring patience is only outweighed by her attention to detail. Carolyn helped shape this book out of a few disparate blog posts, and was instrumental in forming the structure of what you're about to read.

Robert Mills, **Nick Boulton**, and **Benn Pearson** at Mark Boulton Design for project management, typesetting and production.

Steven Teerlinnk for building the backend of the website.

The Britpack, in particular **Andy Clarke**, **Simon Collison** and **Richard Rutter**. **Norm** also gets a nod for never failing to mention the late book every time I spoke to him.

Cameron Moll for his support when he was releasing his own self-published book, *Mobile Web Design*.

The guys at **Beanlogic** for continually listening to me complain about the amount of work to do on this book whilst still trying to hold down the day job.

Last, but certainly not least, to my wife, **Emma**, and daughter, **Alys**, for putting up with me as I spent hours and hours in front of a screen.

Introduction

In the summer of 2005, just before the first @media conference in London, I wrote an article on my blog called 'Five Simple Steps to Better Typography'. It was a five part series and presented some simple facts about typography that I felt needed to be addressed, particularly on the web.

Within two months, the traffic on my site had doubled. In the following months I was Dugg twice, and Slashdotted once, which brought my server to its knees–along with a hefty hosting bill. You might say the articles had taken off somewhat.

After working as a designer solely for the World Wide Web since 1997, I've been aware – sometimes painfully – of the amount of web 'designers' in the industry who haven't been to design school. Don't get me wrong, I'm not presenting some kind of design snobbery here, but the popularity of those articles two years ago highlighted the widespread desire for some basic graphic design tips and techniques that are not generally well known outside of design school.

When I finished school, I attended college to study a two–year course in Art, then on to a Foundation course in Art and Design. The first course after school was well within my comfort zone. We painted, and drew in charcoal, pen and ink. It was art, as I knew it. Foundation was a whole other ball game. I liken it to working in a kitchen, or starting in the army. First off, they tell you to forget everything you've done before. It's a bit melodramatic, but they break you down, and rebuild you from strong foundations.

I went to university in Portsmouth in the UK. It's a small university and had, at the time, one of only two undergraduate typography degrees offered in the UK. Following a higher diploma in graphic design, I wanted to specialise in typography, as I felt there was still much more to learn than in the six months devoted to the subject at university. In Portsmouth I was educated by two book designers approaching retirement. When I arrived, I wanted to learn about type, but on a Mac. I'd spent the summer as an intern at an advertising agency in Manchester, setting tables and forms on an old Quadra. But no, the course in Portsmouth was about the basics.

In the first few weeks, they had us drawing type and grids on a drawing board. I felt more like an architecture student than a typography student. Wasn't I supposed to be working on a Mac? Surely that's what designers need to know?

In the past few years, I've begun to understand the simple lessons I was learning back then. To really get to grips with letterforms, you have to draw them. Even now, I loosely hand-render type in my sketchbook. If the type is a sans-serif, I hand-render a sans serif. If I plan on using Georgia, I hand-render a close approximation.

As design for the World Wide Web is maturing, we are seeing a growing appreciation and willingness to learn good graphic design practice. Studios such as Happy Cog, and Coudal Partners, whose adoption of simple, powerful graphic design as a central service of their offerings, have been influential. Now, three years on, we see a constant chatter about grid systems and good typography. A few people are even art directing.

Simple, sophisticated graphic design is making a shift from the offline world to the web as more designers are finding that the tools which were formerly so constrictive – the browsers – now allow them to create the layouts that once were difficult or impossible. The web is looking good, and will only get better.

Originally devised over three years ago, and announced over two years ago, this book has moved far beyond the original idea of rehashing some old blog posts. Some articles are still included, but mostly, this book has been written from scratch, and is based on the premise that was central to those original blog posts: *Five Simple Steps to Designing for the Web.*

Getting Started

Designing for the web is different than designing for any other medium. The breadth of skills required is sometimes daunting. The depth of experience required, seemingly unobtainable. Yet, the medium attracts designers from all spheres of design practice: from engineering and architecture, to product and graphic design. This chapter aims to provide a snapshot of the current state of the medium, and our role as practitioners working within it.

1

Chapter One
Designing for the web

I regularly receive emails from students and budding designers asking for my opinions and advice on how they can get started in this industry.

'How can I get my first job?', 'What skills do you think I need to land my dream job?', 'If I want to be a web designer, what should I study at school?'. Where do you start? Maybe you're a developer who needs to improve the quality of your design. Maybe you're a print designer who wants a change. Firstly, before making a decision on what course to attend in school, or what software package you need to learn, I believe you need a solid grasp of what the web is today, where it came from and where it might be heading.

Any medium can be defined by its constraints. These constraints effect how a designer is able to work within the medium. To push the boundaries, you need to know where the edges are.

When I started designing for the web I was attracted by the immediacy of the medium. I was a print designer at the time, so this meant I was constrained by print run lead times and the finality of print. Once a job is printed, then that's it, it's printed, finalised, and in the world. With the web, I was able to change things. I was able to evolve the design beyond a deadline. I could tweak, fiddle and redesign – all to my hearts desire. The web created a revolution in graphic design. This was in 1997. What followed was a tidal wave of creative professionals entering the online industry. From writers to graphic designers, we all found the new medium liberating and exciting. The mistake we all made was trying to make the web what it wasn't. We tried imposing other media conventions on technology that it wasn't designed for. A small example of this is HTML tables. HTML data tables are supposed to be for tabular data but, with their cells, rows and columns, they spoke the same visual language of graphic designers who had been using Quark XPress for all those years. They were grids. Before you knew it, every site was made from nested tables and spacer gifs.

The Changing Browser

The browsers are one of the windows by which we consume the web. Web browsers speak to web servers, using a protocol called HTTP, to get and display web pages. When the web first began gathering pace as a medium, several browser manufacturers clambered for the market share. This lead to many of them developing proprietary technologies to handle different media types. The result of this was a proliferation of non-standard code, which lead to increasing problems with interoperability. Through the tireless work of the Web Standards Project, and the W3C, this is all now looking a lot better. The browser manufacturers are listening to the designers and developers and, together with the W3C, are developing towards exciting browser developments, such as font-embedding.

Web browsers are probably the most common way of interacting, searching, playing and communicating on the web. But, increasingly, the web is being accessed by other programs and devices. The once-clear line between online and offline is being continually blurred.

Like many people I know, I use an RSS reader to keep track of the various news sites and blogs I read regularly. An RSS reader isn't a web browser. It's a program that takes RSS 'feeds' and then displays them as a list that you can scroll through and read articles item by item. RSS focusses on delivering content. All style and design is removed, and just the article text is displayed, along with any associated images.

People can of course use email to track their web activity. Through notification emails – from blogs, discussion forums, web applications and services – you can engage with the web. You can track a discussion, reply and participate without ever opening a web browser.

Through something called an API (Application Program Interface), another program can access data on the web, and then display it somewhere else. This brings the web to the desktop. A program I use regularly is Flickr Uploader. It's a small plugin for iPhoto and allows me to upload images from my galleries to my Flickr account online. From there, it can be shared with family and friends. Flickr Uploader does this by using the Flickr API. By adding my account details, Flickr Uploader can 'talk' to Flickr, make sure it's uploading the images in the right place, give them a title and any other meta data, and perform the upload. Again, I haven't opened my web browser to do this.

Up to now, I've only been talking about accessing the web via a computer. Of course, there are several other channels for the delivery of web content – from mobile phones and PDAs to televisions and game consoles.

The iPhone is of particular interest to me (mostly because I own one). Not only is the browser that ships with the iPhone a fully-fledged, fully-featured web browser, but there are an increasing number of iPhone applications that use the web. For example, the Facebook application is so good, I prefer using it to the web browser version. Likewise, with Twitter clients. On my iMac, I use Twitterific – an OS X application – and on my iPhone I use TwitterFon. I hardly ever use a web browser to log in to Twitter.

What I'm trying to illustrate here is the web isn't just limited to Internet Explorer or Firefox. From mobile devices to your Playstation 3, the web is everywhere.

The Changing User

Ten years ago, a lot of people used the web, but the skew was towards a younger, male, technically-savvy audience. Five years later, and adoption had shot through the roof. All sorts of people were using the web to buy gifts or book holiday tickets. Blogging was born, and with it a fundamental change in journalism and how people read news on the web. Now, five years later, my mum is using Facebook. Doesn't that say it all? The web has changed from a publishing medium, to one of tools and applications that enrich people's lives. The audience is now massive and broad-reaching. The technology is getting increasingly pervasive. It's all incredibly exciting! But, with this rapid change, how can we be sure the audience we're designing for today has the same desires, needs and motivations as the audience of six months ago?

The role of research in web design is more important now than ever. By speaking to the potential users of a site and by gathering data on their behaviour, we can then design to their needs. We cannot assume that all users are the same. Just because we, as designers, think a design is appropriate to a given audience, doesn't mean it is. The audience is changing, and we have to keep up.

The Changing Designer

The web moves fast. Really fast. What is new today, will be a convention in six months time. To keep up, a designer not only has to be at the fore-front of current trends and conventions, but also has to be a user of the products and services that define those conventions.

Take Twitter for example. Twitter is a web application that lets you tell other people – who you 'follow', and who 'follow' you – what you are doing. In Twitter's own words:
'Twitter is a service for friends, family, and co-workers to communicate and stay connected through the exchange of quick, frequent answers to one simple question: what are you doing?'

When Twitter first arrived, in 2006/07, I really didn't get it. I had friends I'd keep in contact with via email, and I had a blog for my own expression. Why did I need to use a service like Twitter? For a long time, I didn't use Twitter in favour of using services I was familiar with. Then something started to happen in the bloggersphere – everyone went quiet. 'Weird', I thought. 'Maybe they were all busy. That's it.' Then, over time, respected designers and developers were redesigning their blogs to incorporate postings from these web services and products: Twitter, Flickr, Delicious links, You Tube, Vimeo etc. The blog design became a reflection of the designers 'lifestream'. And, I was missing out on a big discussion. The interesting thing to note is that, recently, I've been working on projects for clients who also want to start incorporating these services. Design conventions are being born, maturing online, and now business is starting to see the benefit. Now, if I wasn't using these products or services, if I wasn't a consumer of the web, I'd be blind to what was possible. It's not enough to rest on your laurels. If you're a web designer, you need to be a web consumer.

I mentioned earlier that it's difficult to keep up sometimes. A web designer's role seems to encompass everything from information architecture, and user experience design, up to front-end development – such as CSS, HTML. Throw in a bit of JavaScript, and a sprinkling of other scripting languages such as PHP, and you get an idea of how broad a web designer's job could be. It wasn't so long ago that every job advertisement for a web designer required most of what I mentioned. I think – well, I hope – that those days are behind us. Modern web design is just too broad a discipline to be moderately good at everything. In fact, I personally wouldn't hire anyone who claimed to do it all – Jack of all trades, Master of none. The web design profession is now splintering into specialisms and this is a very good thing.

Web designers need to be specialists.

Being specialist is difficult when you're a freelancer, or work in a small company. Your boss may ask you to skill up in other fields and diversify. The desire to learn something new can take you spinning off into new directions. But, in the midst of all this, don't lose sight of what your core offering as a designer should be. Mine, for example, could be layout. With my experience, traditional background and my leaning towards typographic design, clients come to me because of that. I have other skills on the periphery – such as knowing how to hand-write HTML and CSS, and project management – but my primary 'selling point' as a designer, would be my knowledge and practice of graphic design layout as applied to the modern web. To lose sight of that would be dangerous – both in terms of running a business, but also in my continued growth of a designer.

A web designer has to be adaptable. Willing to learn, and ready to embrace change. A web designer has to be willing to shed previously high-held design sensibilities and start from scratch. They have to accept, challenge and manipulate the constraints of the web. They must do all of this whilst keeping one eye firmly on their own personal design journey; where they've come from, and where they're going.

All of that is why I love the web. If you give it chance, it's an enriching design medium, and one from which many never return.

Chapter Two
The Job

Working for an Agency

I started out designing for the web whilst working for a small agency in Manchester in the UK. It was 1997, the web was gathering pace, and many small communications studios were dabbling – keen to take advantage of a new medium to 'sell' to clients.

Like me, many designers naturally gravitate towards working in design agencies. Providing a wide variety of work, the smaller agencies offer the designer an opportunity to spread their creative wings. The larger agencies offer the big accounts. With one, you get to make big decisions, the other, you make decisions for big clients – you're very much a cog in a bigger machine. I've worked in both environments, for big agencies and small, and being a designer is different in each.

A big fish in a little pond

Being a designer in a small company is fun. You get to see projects through from start to finish and you're generally involved in all aspects of the design process – from initial concepts through to the finished product. But, with that added breadth in the role, comes more involvement in other parts of the business. You should be willing to get stuck in to all sorts of tasks. In my first job, I was making tea, ordering stationery, phoning couriers, raising invoices etc. I was doing all of this, in addition to my design work.

A little fish in a big pond

I've also worked in a large agency, *AGENCY.COM* - a large, US–based agency of over 500 staff. At the time (1999 – 2001), I worked on accounts for big blue-chip clients such as British Airways and Intel. I ended up being the Senior Art Director on the redesign of the One 2 One website (now T-Mobile). And during that time, not once did I meet a client face to face. This is the single, biggest difference between a large and small agency that has a direct relationship to the work you do every day. Feedback comes third hand from project managers. You have to second-guess the creative brief. You are provided with signed off, prescriptive wireframes that detail every element on the given design – actually leaving little room for any design problem solving. You are a cog in a machine. A worker bee.

For some designers, this is great. The pay–off of working on such accounts far outweighs the disadvantages and frustrations of dealing with account executives, (no offence to account executives intended), and invisible clients. For me, I'm far happier in a working environment where I can make a difference, and that means having contact with my clients.

The In–House Designer

Time with Auntie

Following my stint in London working at Agency.com, my wife and I decided that we'd had enough of the big city and moved to Wales where we both worked at the BBC in Cardiff. It took me a while to get used to it, but working client–side – inside a company or organisation – is a whole different kettle of fish.

I was a member of a small design team, in the end, just two of us would work on the English and Welsh language output of BBC Wales, in addition to some projects for the wider BBC network. There was a lot to do for just two of us. I arrived to the new job, ready to apply what I'd learnt in a busy, global design agency. On my first day, I was given mountains of documentation to read – processes, editorial guidelines, technical guidelines, design guidelines, brand documentation, the list went on and on. Immediately I felt as if the brakes had been applied. Hard.

Different pace, different mindset

I think it took about six months to get used to the change in pace. That was one thing. The other, and most important, change is one of projects and products. As a designer in an agency you become very good at moving from one project to another and from one client to another. You begin to relish the challenge of solving the next problem presented by a client. You thrive on a variety of clients; from telecoms to manufacturing, from startups to blue chip organisations. You don't like working on the same project for very long, as you feel yourself getting stale. But working in–house is all about working on the same project. Sure, you can get smaller projects that make up a whole, but generally you have one client; the company you work for.

At the BBC, I worked on one project for over two years. During that time, there were a lot of smaller projects under that larger project umbrella, but basically, it was the same thing. This required a shift in thinking. Instead of focussing on the next project to come through the door, I began to focus on the 'product', and improving it through incremental change with the rest of my team. This represented more of a move towards product development than web design.

Following my time at the BBC, I feel every designer should, if they can, spend some time working in-house. It has certainly changed the way I approach design.

'I'm not a Designer'

This book isn't just for designers. I'm hoping that some of you will be developers, project managers or journalists. How is design part of your job? Maybe you work in-house and don't have a dedicated designer available to work with you. Maybe you run your own website and do everything from the design to the Wordpress theme.

I've worked with loads of great, talented developers over the years. I've been fortunate to sit next to them, rather than sitting next to designers, and as a result have learnt a lot by osmosis. Most of those developers feel they struggle with the practicalities of design; the craft of design. Sure, they're incredible problem solvers, they can write complex software that solves complex problems in elegant ways. But when it comes to knowing what colour to use, many of them were stumped. I'm hoping this is where this book will be helpful. Graphic design isn't magic. Making typeface choices, knowing what tertiary colour to use with green or how to design a five column grid system. These are all tools. There are general rules you can follow.

Chapter Three
Understanding Workflow

I'm going to talk about the design process a bit later on in this book, but there are certain parts of the process that generally fall outside a designer's role, stuff that happens during a project lifecycle that's useful to know about.

One Mockup or Many?

About eight years ago, I'd moved to Cardiff from London, and worked in a company that predominantly produced design for print. I was part of an expanding web team that produced web sites for clients who came to the agency for print work. It was assumed that web design followed the same process as print design. So, the agency would, as part of their pitch for the work, produce speculative designs and present them. This included designs for the web. Then, upon winning the work, we would generally go back a step and then produce three different design directions for the client to pick their preferred route. This was bad for the client, and bad for the agency.

When designers go through that process, they will always produce a preferred design. They will produce a design that they feel best solves the problem. Any other design produced is just playing lip-service to the process and nothing more. For many years now, following a brief from a client, I've been producing one design and then iterating and amending to improve it. This has several advantages:

- No time is wasted. The process I described would see lots of wasted time – first the speculative work, and then the other two design directions.
- More involvement and understanding from the client. The client is involved earlier in the process. Working iteratively means more contact with them and a shared direction.
- If the design is inappropriate, you can start again without too much time and money being wasted on other design directions.

Design Meets Development

Those of you who work in-house, or even within large agencies, will be well aware of the tensions between designers and developers. In part, these tensions have been created by a lack of understanding by designers early on in the web's history. As I mentioned in earlier chapters, designers thought they could apply print-based design methods and characteristics to web design. We all thought it was fine, but we didn't have to build the sites. Developers would receive the designs and, at the time, despair at the thought of trying to interpret the layouts and create HTML pages. It wasn't until I sat next to a developer for over two years that I began to appreciate the value in communicating with developers as much as possible through the design process.

Corporations spend thousands and thousands of pounds every year trying to achieve efficiency in departments where, in my opinion, a simple seating change would suffice. If you're a designer working in a large agency, do yourself a favour, and don't sit next to other designers. Likewise, if you're a developer, or project manager, sit next to your project team members, not your discipline peers. In two companies that I've worked, we did this. And I continue to share a studio with a web development company. Even if you don't work on projects directly, the shared interests and passions for the web are invaluable at raising the understanding of the two different aspects of web design and development.

The Perfect Design Methodology

There isn't one. There, I've said it. In all of the agencies I've worked, each had their own way of doing things. In the BBC, we tried a few different methodologies, such as Agile and SCRUM, but I'm coming round to the idea that applying a blanket process to every project you work on just doesn't work.

In a large agency, it's important that everyone – from client services, to strategy – understand the web design and development process that is being adopted. That way, when they speak to the client, the client will understand. Having a strong, transparent process is always helpful for clients, too – it puts them at ease. However, for all of this efficiency, transparency and project management rigor, a rigid process is dangerous for any designer or agency.

I take a simple view on this. Every design problem is different, so how can every approach to solve the problem be the same? A cookie-cutter approach to web design and development is about maximising profit and efficiency with minimal innovative and original thinking or problem solving. For example, an architect cannot apply the same design and building process to every building. Various factors determine the approach, from the client's wishes, the local government regulations to the constraints of the building materials. All of this shapes the process and the same can be said for web design. An example of this would be a recent process my studio worked on, the Drupal.org redesign.

The Drupal.org website is primarily a community site representing an ecosystem surrounding the open source content management system, Drupal. Our job was to redesign it. The new Drupal.org would be built and updated by the very community that created it, and to do that, we needed to engage with them in a completely different way. We couldn't adopt a traditional design approach. We needed to bake the community involvement into the process from the very beginning. We did this through many channels:

- Twitter accounts
- Flickr – *for sharing wireframes, logo ideas, and site maps*
- Blogs – *both mine (markboulton.co.uk), and Leisa Reichelt's, the user experience design consultant on the project, (disambiguity.com)*
- Online card sorts
- Remote usability testing
- The Drupal.org website
- IRC
- and a few more...

With this continued involvement from the community, along with iterative design development in the form of weekly prototype releases, there is just no way we could adopt a traditional agency production model. It would have been a disaster and the project would have failed. In this instance, the project defined the process – we were just along for the ride!

Understanding web design and development workflow is as much about understanding the design problem as anything else. Being adaptable to new approaches, to question and revise your approach is as much a part of web design as creating layouts in Photoshop or HTML.

Chapter Four
The Tools

Just like a carpenter, a designer will have his favourite tools.

Just like a carpenter, different designers have different tool preferences. One will like a claw hammer, the other, Photoshop! I, for example, prefer Adobe Photoshop over Adobe Fireworks for creating layouts. I prefer sticky notes and layout pads over Omnigraffle for creating wireframes. I prefer Panic's Coda over Textmate for writing my HTML and CSS. The designer's toolbox could be rammed full of different applications to suit different needs. In fact, many designers continue to search for the perfect application to suit a particular job. What follows in this chapter are the tools I prefer. There is no right or wrong, best or worse – these are just the tools that I have found suit me best.

Pen and Paper

If there's one thing I can be sure of, I'd be completely and utterly lost without a pen and a sketchbook at arms reach. Even now as I type this, I can see three sketchbooks on my desk. You don't need a Moleskine or anything fancy – any sketchbook will do. I often keep several going at a time:

- A Moleskine esque sketchbook – *A5 size, this one goes with me everywhere.*
- An A4 lined notepad. This lives on my desk at work – *mostly for writing ideas down or that kind of thing.*
- An A3 layout pad – *You can buy these in most art and design supply shops. The paper is thin, which makes tracing easy. I tend to do most of my wireframing and large scale sketching on this pad.*
- Little A6 book – *This one stays in my coat pocket. Perfect for jotting down those ideas whenever they may occur.*

Now, I'm fussy when it comes to pens. I can't stand ordinary, cheap ball-point pens, (they leak), or fountain pens, (they leak too). For a while now I've used two types of pen: a Sharpie Twin Tip, (black), and a Pilot V-5 Hi Techpoint. The Sharpie has a thick nib, the Pilot a small nib. They don't leak, and, if you can stand the smell of the Sharpie, they last for ages.

Browsers

One of the challenges of designing for the web is not knowing the user's browsing experience. They could be viewing your carefully crafted design in the latest version of Firefox, or, Internet Explorer 5. There are many browsers for the users to choose from, all with multiple versions, each slightly better than the previous. I'm going to highlight a few here, that I believe are the top browsers, (by usage), in the world today.

Internet Explorer

 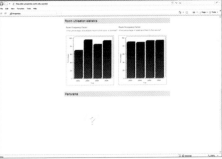

The most ubiquitous browser on the planet, totaling over 68% of the browser market share in 2008 (for versions 4 – 8)* shipped with the Windows operating system, Internet Explorer has been responsible for more wasted development hours, and lost sleep and hair, than perhaps any other browser in the web's relatively short history. Up until version 6, Internet Explorer got a lot wrong, particularly with CSS, that made designing for it a bit of a nightmare. This perpetuated the 'browser sniffing' – where a script in the web page detects what browser the user is viewing the site on, and a different stylesheet is served – that should've died with Netscape 4. Then, along came version 7, and things got a lot better.

Internet Explorer 7 is a lot easier to develop CSS for. It renders styles similarly to its nearest rival, Firefox.

---

* Source: Wikipedia: *http://en.wikipedia.org/wiki/Usage_share_of_web_browsers*

Mozilla Firefox

Firefox is a free, open-source browser managed by the Mozilla Corporation. In its relatively short life, it has cornered a remarkable 21.34% of the market share. It has done this by being available on various platforms – from Mac OS X and Windows, to Linux and other Linux derivatives – and also its unwavering support of Web Standards, and speed of rendering.

Firefox is considered by many designers as their browser of choice – particularly when authoring and testing HTML and CSS. Generally, it gets it right.

* Source: Wikipedia: *http://en.wikipedia.org/wiki/Usage_share_of_web_browsers*

Safari

Safari is Apple's proprietary browser available on Windows, OS X, iPhone and iPod touch, (Mobile Safari).

Opera

Opera is a browser developed by the Opera Software company. It actually does a heap more than just web browsing. You can chat on IRC (Internet Relay Chat), download BitTorrent files or read RSS feeds.

Browser tools and add–ons

Firefox extensions

Web Developer Toolbar is a Firefox add-on that adds a menu and toolbar to the browser to help web designers and developers. It includes some fantastic functionality such as being able to turn on and off styles, use user stylesheets and more.

Firebug is an amazing addition to Firefox. It adds an incredible array of tools to help web design and development whilst you browse around the web. From tweaking CSS on-the-fly, to inspecting DOM elements, it has pretty much everything you should need.

Bookmarklets

XRAY *http://www.westciv.com/xray/*

XRAY is free bookmarklet that 'lets you see the box model in action'. It's a piece of cake to use. Navigate to the page you want to 'XRAY', click the bookmarklet and a little floating window will appear. Now, clicking any element in the browser will review its size, relative position, ID and class, together with any CSS attributes that have been applied to it. It's the perfect companion when bug-fixing CSS.

Desktop Software

When it comes to moving pixels around on screen, I only use a handful of tools that I've used for years. I've been using Apple Macs for fifteen years now, so these tools are predominantly for Apple Macs – although the Adobe tools, and Dropbox, is cross-platform. I keep trying new tools as they come on the market, but these old favourites are never more than a click away.

Adobe Photoshop

Photoshop has been around as long as I've been using Apple Macs. I think the first version I used was version two. Let's put it this way, I've been using Photoshop long enough to remember what a big deal it was when Adobe introduced Layers into version three. I primarily use Photoshop for layout. The introduction of editable text, and functionality like the *Save For Web* option, made designing for the web a lot easier than it used to be. Years ago, I would have sliced images from Photoshop, creating my HTML from the slices. Nowadays, I use Photoshop purely as a layout tool before moving onto creating the layout from scratch in HTML and CSS. It has its quirks, for sure. Its becoming increasingly bloated as Adobe tries to apply the product to a broad industry. It's increasingly unstable as a result – not to mention its uncanny ability to turn the cursor into a spinning beach ball at the drop of a hat. But, all that said, I couldn't bring myself to use anything else. With over fifteen years of using it, for me, using Photoshop is like wearing that old, battered pair of slippers. You know you should probably replace them, but try as you might, you can't bring yourself to do it.

http://www.adobe.com/photoshop

Adobe Illustrator

Illustrator is another software package I've used for a long time, almost as long as Photoshop. It can be used to create incredibly complex illustrations, or, as a website layout tool. I don't use it for layout, but that is more of a habitual thing, rather than a deficiency in the software. I use Illustrator for creating logotypes and logos, illustrations and icons. Basically, any vector artwork.

http://www.adobe.com/illustrator

Adobe Fireworks

Fireworks is worth a mention. Fireworks is aimed at web professionals – it's designed around our needs. For example, the latest version, CS4, has a primary selling point of being able to convert to standards-compliant HTML and CSS for 'Rapid Prototyping'. I used to use Fireworks for a lot of my web production needs when it first came out in 1999, (when it was Macromedia Fireworks). Since Photoshop started to integrate more web-focussed features, I've never gone back to using Fireworks, even though I know a lot of its optimisation is more sophisticated. Its workflow seems to be much improved, and the feature set looks great. But, I keep giving it a try for a day or so, only to go back to what I'm more productive with. To me, Fireworks feels like a new pair of slippers; uncomfortable, different and unfamiliar.

http://www.adobe.com/fireworks

HTML editors

I used to let Dreamweaver create my HTML. That was when I didn't understand, or want to understand the inner workings of HTML. I thought that was a developer's job, not mine. Upon seeing the error of my ways, I started using BBEdit by Bare Bones Software. BBEdit is now on version 9 and is still a superb text editor for the Apple Mac. It allows the creation of 'sites' and auto-complete – amongst other features – and proved to be a perfect replacement for Dreamweaver. I used that until Coda, from software company, Panic, was released a couple of years ago. Coda was like a breath of fresh air. Whereas BBEdit had grown up from Mac OS System 9, and never really felt like a native Apple Mac application, Coda felt every much like a native application. The latest version includes a Terminal right there in the application, and SVN, (Subversion), integration. It's simply a fantastic text editor.

http://www.adobe.com/dreamweaver
http://www.barebones.com/products/bbedit
http://www.panic.com/coda/

Other tools

I use two other applications all the time. For all FTP, SFTP, (Secure FTP), and Amazon S3 transfers, I use Transmit, again by software company Panic. I also use a relatively new software product called Dropbox. Dropbox is simply fantastic. It's free, for 2GB of online storage. It creates a folder in your home directory called 'Dropbox', and everything that you put in there is synced and uploaded to the web. Then, if you have Dropbox installed on another computer, you can have access to it. Dropbox comes into its own when you use it as part of a team's workflow as we've been trialing recently at Mark Boulton Design. We have a couple of employees and contractors working throughout the UK and Europe. To streamline the sharing of documentation, we use a company-wide shared Dropbox. This simple addition has probably increased productivity ten-fold over the past three months of continued use. Another worthwhile mention for Dropbox is that there is version control included. So, if you accidently delete a file, you can go back through history and retrieve it. And it's free, did I mention that?

http://www.panic.com/transmit/
https://www.getdropbox.com/home

In this part so far, I've talked about the various tools I use, some factors that influence design workflow, and the various roles a designer takes within large and small organisations. But many designers either start off working by themselves, or, like me, end up there after several years of working for 'The Man'. In the next chapter, I'm going to outline the steps and discuss the considerations one has to consider if you are planning on working for yourself.

Chapter Five
Working for yourself

So you want to work for yourself? And why not.

You can dictate your own hours, have the freedom to take time off when you want it without getting into trouble from the boss; you can do what you want to do, when you want to do it. At least, that's what I thought when I started working for myself a year ago. I couldn't have been more wrong.

The freedom of being in control is terrifying. The pressure of knowing it really is down to you whether you succeed or fail can weigh heavy.

Where I live almost 400 people a week start their own business. Everybody is different and end up giving it a go for a variety of reasons. However, most of these people share common ground. Things that they need to think about when planning to go it alone.

As I said, I've only been my own boss for a couple of years now, so I wouldn't call myself an expert on this. I can however tell you my story, and the mistakes I made along the way. This section is a bit longer than the previous as, when I was first contemplating going freelance, I had so many questions and practical advice was lacking. Also, this section specifically deals with UK company and Tax laws, but I'm sure, in your country, the rules are similar and can be easily applied. Remember, I'm no lawyer!

Why do it in the first place?

Starting a business is one of the most challenging, but rewarding, things you can do. The reason most people never end up doing it, although I'm sure many would love to, is because they think it takes luck, a clever idea or just knowing the right people. That's not true. It's about you.

Maybe you have a great idea that you just can't keep a secret anymore. Maybe a colleague has approached you to setup a business with them on the back of a contract they've just secured. Maybe you just hate your job and wish you were your own boss. The catalyst is different for everyone.

For many people, including myself, they've found their career takes a certain path where self-employment is the next natural progression. I was working full-time at the BBC as a designer when my enquiries to do freelance work reached such a peak that I was doing two jobs. At that point, one of them had to go before my wife did!

Whatever the reason to set up business, it's a personal one that only you can make.

Do you need a business plan?

A Business Plan is just that; a plan about your business. It's used to look ahead, allocate resources, focus on key points, and prepare for problems and opportunities. It doesn't need to be a scary document that you take months to write. However, some banks, investors, or other funding bodies will insist on a well-written, concise Business Plan on which to base their decisions, so in that sense, it's a very important document.

1. **Executive Summary:** Write this last. It's the summary of the document.
2. **Company Description:** This details how and when the company was formed.
3. **Product or Service:** Describe what you're selling.
4. **Market Analysis:** You need to know your market. Establish the need for your product and why people need it.
5. **Strategy and Implementation:** Be specific. Investors love this stuff. They need to know you have a clear plan of attack.
6. **Management Team:** Include backgrounds of key members of the team.
7. **Financial Plan:** Include a profit and loss account, cash flow breakdown and a balance sheet.

Make no mistake, writing a business plan can be a daunting prospect, but it doesn't have to be great the first time around. A business plan should be revised throughout the business' lifetime – it's not just for startup businesses. I've just gone through my third draft in my first year of business.

Get help

This is perhaps the most important step in setting up your own business. You will realise you can't do it on your own. You will need good advice from the following people:

1. **An accountant:** Preferably a small business specialist.
2. **A bank manager:** All new businesses should be allocated a small business specialist from their chosen bank.
3. **A financial advisor:** You will need the advice of somebody who can assist in the financial direction of the company.
4. **The Government:** Yes, the government can help.

Out of all of these, I'd advise you spend the most time trying to find a really, really good accountant. Many business owners will tell you that a good one is worth their weight in gold. In addition to the usual accounts stuff they can give you invaluable advice.

The different kinds of 'company'

To register as self-employed in the UK, you have to register with the Inland Revenue as one of several company types:

Sole trader

Being a sole trader is the easiest way to run a business, and does not involve paying any registration fees. The downsides are you are personally liable for any debts that your business incurs and, if you do well, you could be paying high income tax.

A Partnership

A partnership is like two or more Sole Traders working together. You share the profits, but also the debt.

A Limited Liability Partnership (LLP)

An LLP is similar to a Partnership. The only difference is the liability, or debt for example, is limited to investment in the company.

A Limited-liability Company

Limited Companies are separate legal entities. This means the company's finances are separate from the personal finances of their owners.

Franchises

A franchise is like a license to an existing successful business.

Social enterprises

This one probably doesn't apply to web development. According to Business Link, Social enterprises are 'businesses distinguished by their social aims.' There are many different types of social enterprises, including community development trusts, housing associations, worker–owned co–operatives and leisure centres.'

The choice of company is something you must do in order to pay your taxes. Speak to your accountant about which will suit your needs better.

How to finance yourself

Before I made the leap into full–time self–employment, I read a lot of articles which said I'd need six months salary in the bank before I went out on my own. Although that is good advice, depending on your salary, that is quite a hefty chunk of cash that will be hard to save.

Like most people, I didn't have that sort of money knocking about so I had to have a close look at cash flow over the first few months of business to ensure I could pay myself. This cash came from several sources.

1. **Money in the bank.**
   I did have some money in the bank. Not a huge amount, but I had some.

2. **Contracts.**
   I had a number of contracts signed and ready to go when I went on my own. These proved invaluable in kick–starting my cash flow.

3. **Funding.**
   There are many funding options available. Grants, loans and private investment. All of them except grants require you to pay them back though, and for that you need a good business plan and an idea of how you're going to pay them back. Grants and small business loans are available from local government bodies for example. I'd advise making an appointment with your local Business Link to discuss your options.

4. **The Bank.**
   Get an overdraft facility. Mostly, even for limited companies, these will have to be personally guaranteed – which means if you default on paying it back then you're personally liable – but they can provide a vital buffer for cash flow in those early days.

5. **Charge up–front.**
   When you get a contract in, especially if it's for fixed cost, then charge a percentage up–front. This will help with the cash flow. If you can't charge up–front, then make sure you charge monthly. Again, it will keep the cash flow nice and happy.

Basic accounting

What is Cash Flow?

Cash Flow is the life blood of your new company. It's the ebb and flow of cash coming in and going out. The aim is to have a positive cash flow, so there is more cash coming in than there is going out once you deduct all your overheads.

You will also need to forecast your cash flow. This is still one of the most sobering things I have to do regularly because it clearly shows the current state of your business. Every month I review my cash flow and I forecast for three months, and for six. I make a list of all the invoices that need to be sent in those two time periods and make sure I'm hitting my monthly and quarterly cash flow targets. Like I say, it can be scary at times.

Tax

There are two types of tax: Income Tax and Corporation Tax. For Sole Traders, Partnerships and LLPs, you will be charged income tax on your profits. That's important, so I'll say it again. You'll only be taxed on your profits. Things like equipment costs, rent, phone and other office expenses are deducted from this.

Limited companies are charged Corporation Tax on their profits. The employees of that company are charged income tax on their income. As with a Sole Trader etc. Limited Companies are only taxed on their profits.

VAT

At the time of publication if your business earns £64,000 or more in a financial year, you have to register for VAT. If you think you might hit that target during the year, you can voluntarily register before hand.

Being VAT registered means you have to charge your customers for VAT on top of your services. Currently in the UK, VAT is 15%. You're in effect collecting taxes for your government. Nice aren't you? One of the advantages of being VAT registered is that you can claim VAT back on purchases for your business, so for example if you buy a new computer, you can claim the VAT back from that purchase.

All this VAT gets added up and you have to pay the government every quarter.

For more information about your obligations as a business to pay your taxes, go to the Inland Revenue website. There are some great tools on here to help you – you can even file your tax return online.

Establishing a customer base

Prior to starting my own business, I worked full time. As a designer, or developer, you will probably get enquiries to do freelance work in your spare time. This is the time to start building up your customer base whilst you still have the security of a full-time job. Sure, it means burning the candle at both ends, but it does ensure a smoother transition from employed to self-employed.

Schmoozing

A good way to drum up business is to network. This can be done traditionally, such as Business Club lunches and events organised by your local authority. One of the most effective ways of getting your face known is by attending the many web conferences, workshops and meetups going on throughout the world. From learning events such as An Event Apart and Web Directions North to the larger conferences such as SXSW and IA Summit, they all provide a great platform to meet people in the industry who may require your services.

Contribute and Interact with your market

If you're a design studio that designs websites but has a strong focus on User Experience design, write a company blog about that subject. If you write interesting content, and give it away free, then traffic to the site will increase as will your page rank in Google. This means that if a potential client searches for User Experience, they will get your site in their search results and there is a clear path into your site from some quality content.

Giving a little quality content away for nothing may make the difference in landing that next big project.

Making the switch from being employed to self-employed

The power of the Day Job

If you're employed, but planning to go freelance, then keep your day job for a while. Secure some freelance projects to work on in your spare time, but use the cash that generates as a buffer for when you go it alone. Make sure the two worlds don't collide though. Keep your boss happy in work, but now is the time to be a bit of a jobsworth. Get in on time, leave on time, take an hour for lunch – do everything you can to maximise the time you have available to work on the freelance projects.

A smooth transition

Working two jobs is hard, and you won't be able to keep it up for long. This stage in starting up your business is perhaps one of the most difficult. The aim is to ensure a smooth transition from being employed to self-employed. You will need some cash in the bank and a few contracts for your first couple of months of being on your own. The hard thing is keeping your current boss happy in the process. It's not easy.

There are a number of great job boards that advertise design and development projects regularly. The two I've used successfully in the past to drum up some business are the 37Signals Job Board, and Cameron Moll's Authentic Jobs.

How to achieve long term success

Keep one eye on the future

Forecasting business can be quite difficult. How will cash flow look in three months time? Are you saving enough money for the end of year tax bill? To succeed in business I think you need one eye on the present and one eye fixed firmly on the future. The short-term future. Whilst it's great to have dreams and aspirations for your new business, that shouldn't be at the expense of ensuring you have enough work coming in over the next six months.

Customer service

Remember if you're a designer or developer, you're providing a service. We're in a service industry and with that comes Customer Service. I know it may sound a bit trite, but treat clients as you would like to be treated. Treat them with respect and never lose sight of that fact that they are paying the bills.

Ten things I wish I'd known

10. Wearing many hats

Before I set up business, I'd read a fair few 'how to' books and a number of blogs that talked about the many roles you would have to adopt whilst running your new business. I still struggle with it.

On a typical day I am a designer, a project manager, a salesman and a book-keeper. Each role requires a different mindset and it can be very difficult to switch between them.

9. Home is for home things

Keep work and home separate. When you work at home, this can be difficult. When I had my workplace in my house, I made sure it was a completely different room which was furnished like an office–not just your spare room with a desk in it. One tip which worked for me: wear your shoes during the day, when you're working, and at night, take them off. It's a silly little thing, but you will soon associate shoes with work. So, when you take them off, that's home time.

8. What goes around comes around

Be nice to people. Business doesn't have to be unpleasant. Treat people how you expect to be treated. Be fair, professional and above all, polite.

7. Don't take on too much

This one is a killer. I still do it and probably will for many years to come. When you don't have any work booked in in three months time, the tendency is to get more work in now with the hope that, financially, you'll be more stable in the months you don't have work. It makes sense, but you end up working too hard. As a result, quality dips, customers get a bad service and, over time, your business will dry up.

6. Hire somebody before you need to

I've recently had this problem. I've been so busy recently that I needed help. After hiring someone, I realised I'd been in this position for too long. I needed help about three months before I thought I did.

5. Don't under-charge

Work out your costs on an hourly, or daily, basis and then add 30%. It covers costs and, until you get the hang of it, you're probably under-charging anyway. I was.

4. Confidence

Remember, you're the expert. You're not doing this job because you're average at it. If a customer wants to buy your product, or hire you, it's because you're good at what you do.

3. Customer Service

If you're a web designer or developer, unless you're producing and selling a product, you will be providing a service. With a service comes Customer Service and, yes, customers are always right.

2. Accounting Software

I was using a homemade system coupled with an Excel spreadsheet for my accounting needs. As the business grew, I needed something a little robust. I wish I'd learnt Sage or something sooner because now I don't really have the time.

1. Plan for tomorrow

I have three to-do lists. A Month list, a Three Month and a Six Month. Each list has a bunch of things I need to do for that time period. This allows me to have short, mid and long term goals. I class Six Month as long term here as, in this industry, I believe you need to be adaptable and can't really plan for more than six months in advance.

Wrapping up

Making a leap of faith is the first step to starting a business. However, for your business to grow and flourish, you will need much more than faith. First off, you must have upmost confidence in your ability to make it work. You need to be aware of the risks, but not scared to death by them. You'll need to have good organisational skills, flexibility and a high degree of commitment. Most of all, you need to have fun and love what you do.

Timeline: Six months to taking the plunge

January

6 Months to go
Start building a customer base. Trawl the freelance websites, (job boards – authentic jobs etc), and get yourself a few freelance gigs. Register your business with the Inland Revenue, (see section on deciding what business you should be). I'm afraid for the next six months, you'll be working two jobs. If you can get funding for your venture, start researching what you can get and when.

February

5 Months to go
Continue to get those freelance gigs in. Begin to research a good local accountant. Book an appointment with several banks – you'll need to get a business bank account – but it's worth shopping around. Have meetings to discuss funding opportunities.

March

4 Months to go
Found a good accountant? Right, you need to have a meeting with him/her regarding your new venture. Finalise your bank account with your chosen bank. Continue to build up your customer base. Now is the time to speak with some local companies to see if they need freelance help. Are you going to be working from home? If not, you need to start looking for somewhere to work from.

April

3 Months to go
You should be getting some money in from your freelance gigs by now. Save it–you might need it in a few months.

May

2 Months to go
You should be working like a dog now and really looking forward to working for yourself. At this stage, everything should pretty much be in place for you to make that smooth transition from employed to self-employed.

June

1 Month to go
Hand in your resignation. If possible, try and get some work booked in for the first three months of being on your own. Make sure you also get paid by these clients monthly so cashflow isn't an issue.

Research & Ideas

How would you answer the question: 'What is design?' Do you imagine that it's primarily an act of creativity, perhaps something beautiful that an artist might produce? Do you think that it's more a question of technical issues and accuracy?

While good design invariably has an eye on aesthetics and a concern for technical accuracy and perfected details, graphic design, (whether for the web, print, or screen), is essentially about solving problems. Each project has its own set of unique problems to address. What is the first step in problem solving? You begin with research. You immerse yourself in the needs of the client, audience/readership, and the project itself, and become as informed as you can be.

Like most people, I often struggle to envisage original, effective ways to solve the problems presented by each project. This struggle has many causes: a complex or ill-defined brief, lack of constraints, or an environment or process that, rather than inspiring creative thinking, deadens or impedes the idea-generating part of your mind. This section aims to help you overcome these obstacles.

We'll go through the design process step-by-step, look closely at how research helps you generate those brilliant new ideas you promised, and spell out how to move smoothly from the initial problem- as the client presented it to you-to something you'll be proud to put in your portfolio. We'll also look at tools that make it all easier, ones I've used almost daily over the past few years to help me as I work.

2

Chapter Six
The Design Process

Before delving into design principles for the web, let's look at the traditional design process which I was taught in school–still the standard in use today by the graphic design industry.

The Traditional Design Process

1. Brief

The brief is comprised of a couple of documents:

The client brief is what the client gives you. It might be a formal Request For Proposal (RFP), or simply a short email. It generally outlines the initial aims and objectives of the project, the deliverables, and may indicate many of the client's expectations about the final work's function or appearance. Deliverables include documents, content, sketches, everything that the client will provide to you and anything that you'll provide to them. The client may also provide deadlines for each deliverable, though whether they deliver theirs on time is a long, sad tale we'd need to cover in a separate book.

The creative brief is a document produced by a designer in response to the client brief. Sometimes, it is an oral brief given at the start of the project by a senior creative, meaning someone on the design team, such as an art director, creative director or designer. It outlines the creative elements of the project. In order for the designers to focus on their part of the process, this is the only document they tend to see.

Already, in this first stage of the process, you can begin to see the cracks. The designers are being separated from the process. They're given their own brief. Why is that? Are designers not capable of extracting that information from the client, the client's RFP, or even from researching the project directly? Design, as we'll see, is not a process that exists in isolation. The job of design isn't just to make information look pretty or to decide if an element on a page should be blue or orange.

It may involve deciding where on a page to place an element, (such as a heading or image), how much emphasis should be given to that element, and how to emphasise it. It looks at readability and how to most effectively arrange information. Good design arises from the initial problem, goals, audience or readership needs, and business plans, and reflects the identity and brand of the client. Clearly, bringing in the designer as a type of decorator after all the important decisions have been made is not the smartest approach.

2. Research

Research is vital to the success of any design solution. A designer should be as informed as they can be about the project.

Research can be conducted in a number of ways, many of which I'll discuss in detail later in this section. The findings of this research provide three key deliverables in the design process:

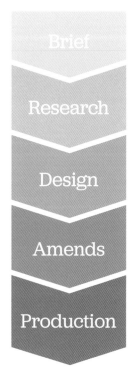

1. Insights to help generate ideas for the design.

2. Data with which to 'sense-check' design solutions. An example of this would be research that led to the generation of project personas, or pen portrait's.

3. Frame the design solution in the real world. Solutions to design problems can often be developed in a bubble. As such, they can quickly become divorced from reality.

Designers don't need to be involved in the actual research, but they do need access to the results. Quite often, research is compiled into a debrief document by a research agency who has been commissioned to conduct the research.

3. Design

The designers get to work. First, they sketch up ideas, which the senior creative's on the team approve, reject or discuss. Ideas are shortlisted, and sense-checked against the Creative Brief before they are worked up to a final solution. This is then presented to the client.

4. Amends after amends after amends

The designers then spend time amending the design to reflect the changes or problems highlighted by the client–sometimes endlessly. I've lost count of the number of times that I've spent needlessly making changes to a design because of miscommunication further back in the process in conversations between people at meetings to which the actual designers were not invited. More often than not, the problems arise because the expectations of either party have not been managed properly.

5. Production

The designers now have to make the design solution into a product – be it a brochure, some vehicle livery, or a website. This is, once again, a frequently painful point in the process. More often than not, it's because questions have not been answered during the previous stages.

You can see that this linear design process is fraught with potential for going completely wrong – and it does, much of the time. Offices around the world have closets full of unfinished, unpublished projects and hours of work that produced nothing more than arguments and disappointment. The fault often lies with miscommunication between project managers, account executives and designers and it still goes on every day in design and advertising agencies all over the world.

Out with the old, in with the new

I'm not saying I have a better approach, but I've spent enough time shoe-horned into these unworkable processes to have an informed opinion on how they can be improved for both the designer and the end-product. I use a process whose focus is research, ideas generation and iteration.

Like designing for print, or designing products, designing for the web is a somewhat linear process. But with all its hyperlinks, moving parts, usability and accessibility issues, frequent content updates, sometimes by a large number of authors, and a wide variety of users who may be visiting the site for a whole spectrum of reasons, the web design process can be much less directly linear than other forms of design. The website design process is best described, (and conducted), as a series of iterative stages, incorporated into an overall linear process, similar to product design.

The web design process follows the more traditional route closely, but frequently with the addition of these offshoots and cycles of iteration before moving onto the next phase of development. One clear distinction between the traditional route and good web design is that testing is almost always missing from the former but used frequently, or even continuously, in the latter.

The Web Design Process

1. The Brief

As with the traditional process, the web brief should usually be comprised of a few documents:

1. **Client Brief**: This brief is written by the client and is usually the first document produced.

2. **Technical Brief**: This can be produced by the client or agency (or freelance designer). It sets out the technical requirements and scope for the website project.

3. **Creative Brief**: This is produced by the agency in response to the Client Brief. It is used as a central document for the creative phase of the project.

4. **Idea Brief**: This brief – discussed in detail in the next chapter – is a short document, (in fact no longer than a couple of sentences), produced after a period of consultation with the client. It aims to clearly describe the project and is used as a springboard for ideas in the idea generation phase.

During this phase, it's the designer's job to:

Interrogate the client's brief •

Ask questions •

Change and re-define the brief •

Get to the root of the problem that • must be solved

Produce the final Idea Brief •

2. Research & Insights

As with the traditional process, the designer or creative team should conduct research. For a web project this could include the following:

- **Page Impressions** – *a request to load a single page of an internet site.*
- **Unique Users** – *the number of individual users to a site over a defined period, often a month.*
- **User Flows** – *a diagram showing a user's journey, used to show most likely user experience.*
- **Personas** – *fictitious characters that are created to represent the different user types within a targeted demographic that might use a site or product.*
- **Use Cases** – *a description of a system's behaviour as it responds to a request that originates from outside of that system.*

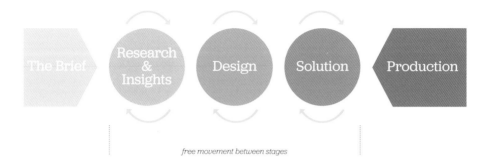

free movement between stages

These should be coupled with more traditional ways of gathering data such as:

- **One-on-One** – *person to person interviews with specific questions asked by the interviewer to gain a specific understanding of the interviewee's behaviour/thoughts associated with a service or product.*
- **Focus Groups** – *a form of qualitative research in which a group of people are asked their thoughts on a product, service, or concept.*
- **SWOT Analysis** – *a strategic planning tool used to evaluate the Strengths, Weaknesses, Opportunities, and Threats involved in a project.*
- **Questionnaires** – *a research instrument consisting of a series of questions and other prompts for the purpose of gathering information from respondents.*
- **Market Segmentation** – *groups of peoples or organisations sharing one or more characteristic that causes them to have similar product needs. E.g. location, age, gender, or socioeconomic status.*

If you're lucky enough to have access to all these types of data and tools, you can begin the project extremely well informed. Even if you only have a few of these, you can still gain much insight about the audience. Whilst data is important in research, it's the insights that you will get, based on the data, that will lead to a successful design solution.

3. Ideas Generation

Calling this the Ideas Generation stage simply formalises what a designer does in any process. In college, I was taught to sketch out my ideas – to move from one brush-stroke to another quickly. The aim was to get as many ideas down in as short a time as possible – not to stop and judge or analyse, but just to make marks.

Ideas for website designs should be treated the same way. Have the idea, write it down, and then move on to the next one. Don't judge, analyse or criticise them – that will come later. This frees you to be experimental, to step outside of 'the box', to be subjective, (or, at times, even more objective), inventive, original and fearless.

The ideas could be generated in the following ways:

- Mark-making and Sketchbooks
- Mood Boards
- Mind Maps
- Ideas Sessions

Everyone is involved in the Ideas phase. The client will have a more informed view of their customers, (though surprises may come later with user testing), so their contributions are essential. The project management team should be involved, as should the designers. The aim is to generate ideas and several heads are better than one. One warning: Be sure to identify this to everyone as just the Ideas Phase, not a decision-making phase. Later, when decisions are made, you'll discover that 'design by committee' is a direct path to a mediocre website. By the time everyone on the committee has strongly influenced the colours, the functions, the placement of content, and every other detail, you'll be left with a lifeless, senseless, overloaded site, and a powerful headache.

The Idea Brief is used as a springboard to help generate those ideas. It's a central point of reference and could be something as simple as 'We want to make our gardening website more engaging for a younger audience'. You'll be thankful for it when clients or others on the team make suggestions that aren't congruent with the final Idea Brief. Does someone suggest stilted language or dull colors? You can just point to the Idea Brief to remind them of the track you've all agreed on.

4. Solution

The results from the Ideas Phase, along with the brief and the research data, are compiled to create a clear design direction.

Lo Fi

This could be a sketch of the page-types, wireframes done in Visio, or an HTML prototype. The point is to get something sketched out, in as complete a state as possible, and begin to solve those problems as they arise. The aim is to do it quickly, and cheaply.

Test and Iterate

Once you've got something that you're happy with, the next stage is to test those results. Testing can be done formally at a usability lab, or in more guerilla fashion with colleagues, friends or family. The point is to get a real person using this lo fi product. That could validate any problem areas.

Design Comps

Design visuals of key pages are done in this phase. They can be produced in tandem with the lo fi work and should be as iterative. The difference is, the Design Comps focus on elements such as brand, colour & typography. They are not being done in isolation from any usability or interaction design though – in fact, the same designer can be working on both the lo fi and Design Comps.

5. Production

Now we're getting into factory mode. The heavy thinking has been done and the project now turns towards realising the project goals: building a website.

The Design Comps should be completed and signed off early in this stage. They should represent a cross-section of the site and form the basis of the unique templates that need to be produced.

The lo fi prototype now needs to be scaled up to a full production model. This is where it's important that the iterative development of the prototype stays as close as possible to the Design Comp process. The last thing you need, so late in the day, is a huge gulf between the visuals the client has signed off and the prototype you've produced internally.

That very problem – which happens a lot – is a symptom of there not being enough collaboration. Designers need to work alongside as many disciplines in the process as possible,

particularly project managers, account executives, writers and –
most importantly – developers. Design and development should
happen at the same time following the Ideas Phase. All the pieces
are in place for each discipline to pick up and run with.

One Of Many Ways

The design process, regardless of final delivery medium, pretty
much follows the same path: Brief, Research, Ideas, Solution,
Production and finally, Product. The web design process I've
described here follows those top-level headings, but has slight
deviations and is leaning towards the design aspects of
the process.

There are many variants to the process of designing for web.
Some advocate a larger proportion of time dedicated to the
research phase–the findings of which inform the production of
lo fi prototypes. Others focus on the design phase, particularly
if the user experience of a brand is high on the agenda. The
process is the same, but the outcome is slightly different. Each
phase of the process grows or shrinks to accommodate the
project requirements or the working preference of the agency
or individual. Many development companies, and in larger
organisations with in-house teams–prefer an agile development
process, such as Scrum. Agile development is a useful process for
developing products or applications, but can be resource-heavy
which makes it difficult to work in a commercial environment.

The important thing to take away from this chapter is there is no
right way to designing a website. Try different methods and find
what suits you and the project.

Chapter Seven
The Brief

The Brief, in its different forms, represents the start of a project and a point of reference throughout a project's life cycle.

Most of the time though, the first brief you will get from a client will be inadequate. It will have vital information missing, it will be focussed internally on the clients business, there will be a lack of focus, and almost always the budget will be omitted. Sometimes, they even provide you with a solution! Clients don't make it easy for us. But, it's not their fault. Nine times out of ten, they will never have written a brief before. Have you?

How do you write a good brief? What's involved in creating the four briefing documents discussed in the previous chapter?

The Client Brief

This is the initial brief from a client. Sometimes, it's just a phonecall or an email. If you're lucky, you might get a comprehensive RFP including preliminary research results and detailed budgets and timescales, but this is the exception rather than the rule.

Most of the time, regardless of complexity, an initial brief is like a handshake. It's an introduction. Some of the time, the client is just looking for validation from you that they've produced a document that you will find useful in getting a price to them.

As with all handshakes, unless you want to be seen as rude, they should be reciprocated. It's important to note that receiving a brief from a client is the start of a conversation.

The Technical Brief

This brief is almost always invisible, unless you request it specifically. Sometimes, it's found in amongst a Functional Specification document, or as part of an RFP. If you aren't supplied one, I suggest you try and create one from whatever sources you can. Discuss it with a client and take pieces from the client brief – even if it's just a quick note on what browsers you're going to develop for, or what backend the system is going to run on.

The important thing is to begin to draw a line in the sand as to what development is being done and to cover your back to some extent.

The Creative Brief

If you're heading up a large team – a senior designer, or team leader for example – then you will need to extract information from the Client Brief in order to brief your team on the job at hand. It falls on your shoulders to create this brief from scratch.

Typically, writing a Creative Brief involves asking the client questions and speaking to a lot of people about different aspects of the project. For example:

- Are there any brand guidelines to adhere to? If so, who's the brand guardian?

- Will you be building the website, or is the client doing it in-house?

- Who will be signing off design on the client-side?

- Who will be responsible for feeding back comments and amends?

- Who are the people involved in the project on the agency and client side?

- Is there any research available?

The aim is to get together a working document with which to:

- Brief your team

- Refer to throughout the project to check you're on the right creative track.

The Idea Brief

The Idea Brief is a sentence that describes the project aims. A good Idea Brief is a problem statement looking for a solution. It's used as a springboard for having ideas in Ideas Sessions (or Brainstorms).

An Idea Brief is sometimes the most difficult to write. It needs to be short, concise and open. Good starting points for Idea Briefs are:

- 'How to...'
- 'We want to...'
- 'How do we...'

They start the sentence off in the right way – by asking a question. It's the designer's job to come up with the answer.

The Right Pair of Briefs

So, you have your four documents, (or maybe, they're just discussions and scraps of paper at the moment – that's ok, they don't have to be manicured documents), now what do you do? Chances are, the brief is still going to be way off something that is actionable. Why? Well, let me introduce you to my briefs to explain all.

Flowery Briefs

A flowery brief uses langauge that no one can understand. It's full of acronyms and abbreviations. There is no focus, but an emphasis on trying to impress the reader with over-complicated terms. It winds this way and that, and then, like an episode of LOST, abruptly stops leaving you with a head full of questions.

Woolly Briefs

Woolly briefs are vague and lacking specifics. Whilst they're better than a Loose Brief, they will still provide little insight into the direction of the project. They leave too much to the imagination.

Tight Briefs

A tight brief is the opposite of loose. Restrictive and too focussed, they spell out the requirements and provide a solution. It's then left to the designer to just implement them. Depending on the client, these are the worst kind of brief to receive – unless your design matches the clients perceived solution exactly, then they're not going to be pleased. If one of these lands on your desk, think twice about taking it on.

Loose Briefs

Loose Briefs are too open and not focussed. 'I want you to give me ideas' would be the classic first line of someone giving you a loose brief. Worse still, they generally end there.

Ideal Briefs

The ideal brief is a brief that isn't too loose, or too tight. It's not woolly, or flowery, but fits just right. It is open enough to facilitate the creation of the other briefs, particularly the Idea Brief. It is clear, and uncluttered.

The Funnel of Focus

The Funnel of Focus is an important visualisation aid in further defining a brief. Imagine a funnel: wide at the top and narrow at the bottom. At the top, is the 'blue–sky' thinking–purely conceptual. At the bottom is specific, focussed thinking. Somewhere in the middle is the place for the ideal brief.

A brief may start at either end of the Funnel. With definition, it could travel up, or down, to that centre point. You're after a brief that is tight enough to be clear, but loose enough to be able to be used as a springboard to create the Idea Brief and Creative Brief.

Conceptual
Non Specific

Ideal Brief

Specific
Focussed

Chapter Eight
Research

Research is a profession in its own right, but it's also an aspect of design that is vital to the success of any design solution.

My wife is an Audience Researcher for the BBC, so it's a profession I'm close to and have a fairly good grasp of its importance. In addition to the type of research my wife does, there is another type of research that should be done by a designer on an almost daily basis: visual research. Combining professional research, with a designer's visual research, can create solid foundations on which to build ideas.

Asking Questions

Successful design solutions are successful business solutions. The first priority in any design task is to understand the business behind the product or website for which you are providing a service. As a designer, you need to understand the company that hired you and the business they are in.

You can get this information from several sources: reading strategic documents and whitepapers; the company's Annual Report, (that is a good one!), or, what I've found most valuable in the past, interviewing key stakeholders.

First of all, you need to find out who those people are. If it's a one-man-band you've been hired by, then it's just them. If it's a bluechip organisation, you need to understand the pecking order. For example, you've been hired by a large energy provider to provide consultancy on the redesign of their website. Their web team is comprised of members from multiple departments – each responsible for different business output: Marketing, Press and Communications, Corporate, HR etc. This could be a large team, and it probably wouldn't be cost-effective, or necessary, to interview all of them. You will need to establish key members of this team, but remember, the client can help you out with this one.

Interviewing the right people

It might be a little too formal to call these discussions interviews. In my experience, they are more like chats–it's a time to build trust and rapport with a new client. A more informal approach puts you and the client at ease and you're more likely to gain some valuable insight if everyone is having a pleasant time!

Market Research

Market research is the collecting, analysing, and reporting of data or information that affect customers, products or services. It's a huge, specialised field. However, anyone can do market research – you don't need to be a recognised member of the Chartered Society of Marketing. With something as simple as a web–browser and Google, you can conduct your own research.

The difficulty with just searching for stuff on Google, or asking your grandmother to do some usability testing for you, is the information gathered might not be accurate or representative. If it's not accurate, or trustworthy, you're already off to a shaky start in gathering information for your ideas. There is a bewildering array of techniques and methodologies that enable the professionals to provide us with accurate research.

As a designer, I've had to read market research agency results and briefing documents as part of a research phase. They can provide vital insight, but, for a long time I found the terminology confusing. I didn't have a clue what they were talking about and I was too embarrassed to ask. Anyway, after years of cobbling my way through documents, I'd like to give you a head start and list some of the terms and definitions.

Qualitative Research

Qualitative research is a type of research conducted to establish the audience's beliefs, feelings, motivations and triggers. Results are often rich in insights.

Quantitative Research

Quantitative research is a type of research that provides valid data. It's all about the numbers. Insights can be difficult at times, as quantitative research requires analysis to identify trends.

Primary Research

Primary research is new, not old, information.

Questions to ask during stakeholder interviews.

- Describe your products or services
- What are your three most important business goals?
- Who is your target market?
- What makes you better than your competition?
- How do you market your product or service?
- What are the trends that may affect your industry in years to come?
- Is there any impending, or current, legislation that will affect your business?
- If you could communicate a single thing about your company, what would it be?

Secondary Research

Secondary research is research performed on old data. E.g. New analysis on data gathered last year.

Segmentation

You hear a lot about 'Market Segmentation'. It means the market of the product, or service, is segmented into groups. Those groups, or segments, represent a part of the customer group or audience. They are usually grouped by demographics such as sex, age, ethnicity, income, occupation etc.

Focus Groups

Focus groups are moderated group discussions whose participants are selected to accurately represent the audience or customer.

Task–Based Usability Testing

Users of a website are asked to complete a task whilst being observed. The people tested are selected to accurately represent the audience or customer.

Visual Research

Visual research is the gathering of visual information, stuff that a designer will find useful in solving the problem. Visual research is generally the domain of the designer, or the project team, rarely the client.

Sketchbooks

Since being in art college nearly twenty years ago now, I've always kept sketchbooks. They're places where I keep my doodles and ideas – where I'm free of judgement. A place where it's okay to make a mistake. A sketchbook is a vital tool for a designer – I really can't stress that enough.

A designer's sketchbook is not so different from an artist's. If you opened an artist's sketchbook, it's probably full of sketches, paintings, doodles and studies. If you open a designer's sketchbook, there will be doodles and drawings, but the studies will be written. There will be notes – sometimes pages and pages of the written word punctuated by small diagrams.

Designers tend to think visually. Sometimes, these sketchbooks are works of art in their own right. They're treasured tools of a designer's trade and generally follow them everywhere. But there lies a danger. Designers need to take heed – sketchbooks are just tools – not diaries. They should form part of the research of a project just as a market research document should. They shouldn't be precious.

If you're new to design, or maybe you fell into web design from another discipline, then try keeping a sketchbook for a couple of months. Instead of using sticky notes, or till receipts for recording those moments of inspiration, jot it down in your sketchbook. If you see some nice type on a flyer whilst you're out and about, stick it in there. You'll be surprised at how quickly it fills up with interesting and relevant visual information.

Virtual Sketchbooks

If you work all day on the web like me, then it's not very environmentally friendly, or cost-effective, to take a screengrab of something, print it out and then stick it in your sketchbook. This is where applications such as iPhoto, or Flickr are invaluable.

If, whilst browsing around, you see something that you fancy, then grab it and pop it into Flickr, or iPhoto. Start building a virtual sketchbook. Many people have already started to do this on Flickr and it's proving to be a great resource for doing visual research. Take the typography pool for example. It's jammed full of really great photographs of typography from all over the globe, and it's updated daily. Where else could you get this information? It's a fantastic resource.

Flickr is a great way to keep a visual sketchbook on the go using iPhone app, **Airme**

Moodboards

Moodboards are created specifically for a project. The aim is to present a visual language on one sheet of paper. For example, let's say you were designing a website for a builders- merchants. To establish the overall feel of the visuals for the site, you might go and print out a lot of competitor's websites and couple that with some material from related trades. The material could include images, photography, colour, typography, layout, illustration or patterns. Anything visual to build up a language.

These scraps of paper, (or digitally if you prefer), would then be stuck on a piece of paper to give an overall impression of the proposed visual language for the new website.

Gaining Insight

So, you've got all this stuff, now what do you do with it? Remember, for a designer, the aim of the research is to provide insight. Insights that will act as springboards when you come to generating ideas.

Start to focus in on the research by applying some lightweight analysis. A good tool to use to focus in on the problem, is one which marketeers use called the SWOT analysis. Strengths, Weaknesses, Opportunities and Threats. Strengths are the strengths of the current product or service. Weaknesses are where it falls down. Opportunities are how you can make it better, and Threats are those things that could undermine its success. It's a simple tool that can be extremely effective in providing simple, top-level research that is, above all, easy to understand by the whole team.

Once you've established some insights, and these might be as simple as two or three word sentences, you need to record them and stick them on a wall or something. Insights can only act as springboards for ideas when they are presented in isolation from the rest of the other research material. Now we can start to have some fun.

Chapter Nine
Ideas

Ideas. They're at the heart of every creative process. However, almost no really good ideas are flashes of inspiration. They may start that way – a single glimmer of something special – but in order to work, they need to be honed.

They need time spent on them. You see, the 'flash of inspiration' idea, (the Eureka moment), is only part of a longer process that, if ignored, will see most ideas simply fizzle out. So, how do you 'have' ideas? Sit about and wait for them to pop into your head? If only most of us had the luxury to do so. No, for most designers, ideas have to be squeezed out of us every day. To stand up to this challenge, designers need to arm themselves with some good tools.

Creative Thinking

When I receive a brief, along with research, I try and formulate an Idea Brief, (if I haven't received one already). As discussed earlier, an Idea Brief is a sentence, or two, that will sum up the project and frame it as a problem statement. Something like:

> 'We need to redesign our News service to appeal to a more global audience'

or

> 'How do we engage an older audience for our social networking product?'

This simple sentence is the question you are trying to answer and should be referred to throughout the process of having ideas.

I start out the ideas process on my own, with my sketchbook. I take myself away from my every-day working environment to somewhere with a comfy chair and an endless supply of tea (yes, a teashop). I generally sit there for a while staring into space.

Most of the time, nothing happens until I start doodling. As I start making those initial marks, then more will follow and I'll start taking notes. The key here is to move from one idea to another quickly. If you think something works – and you will get these ideas where you think 'that's it, I've solved it' – then park it, and move on to the next.

Inspiration

Inspiration is a completely subjective thing: One person's junk, maybe another person's pet project. Coupled with insights, inspiration is the other half of generating ideas. You can get inspiration from all sorts of places. Many people find music inspiring for example, or a long walk by the beach. Pieces of inspiration are like the springboards of insights of idea briefs: they send you off in directions that haven't yet been explored.

Inspiration
- Mass culture
- Pop culture
- World culture or heritage
- Poetry
- Colours
- Symbols
- Metaphors
- Values
- Dreams
- Television
- Music
- Art
- History
- Analogies
- Sounds
- Science
- Technology
- Myths
- Legends

I tend to find inspiration in a lot of things. Actually, I've got a confession to make, I'm a terrible hoarder of all sorts of printed stuff. Wherever I go, I always seem to come home with a newspaper, a flyer or two or some photographs of some signage or typography I've seen. My wife has asked on several occassions why I need all this stuff. 'You only end up putting it on a shelf and never looking at it again'. Probably true, but it's not the 'thing' that I'm interested in – it's what's on it. That gets looked at, the inspiration that that gives generally springboards my imagination off somewhere else – they're useful objects.

At @media 2007, a web conference in London, Jon Hicks, (of Hicksdesign), gave a presentation on 'How to be a Creative Sponge'. It was a lighthearted look at how designers can gain, catalogue and store inspiration from all sorts of sources. One in particular stood out for me – it turns out I'm not the only one who has a taste for flyers. Jon described the flyer stands you find in theatres, cinemas and information centres as an 'all you can eat buffet' of inspiration. Next time you're out, just have a look over one of these stands. See if there is any visual style you can draw inspiration from in one of your designs.

Structured Ideas

As I said earlier, it's not enough to rely on those sparks of inspiration for ideas. Most of the time, they have to be worked at. Luckily we have one good tool to help us with that: Brainstorming, or Ideas Sessions as I like to call them.

Ideas Sessions

The Rules of Brainstorming

All ideas are equal •
We're here to have lots of ideas •
No Judging •
Analyse the ideas later •
Everyone's equal (no pulling rank) •
Have fun •
Keep to time •
One idea at a time •

Ideas Sessions are group activities that take place with key members of the project team. This is important. In order for the ideas to be taken seriously, they need buy-in from the people who matter, namely the CEO, or Marketing Director. Without that internal buy-in on the client side, an idea, no-matter how great, will almost always fail.

Another important member of an ideas session is the facilitator. They should be trained in creative facilitation and are there to coax and squeeze the best ideas the team has to offer.

A typical running order of an ideas session would be:

1. Attendees – *get them to bring a random object*
2. Reveal the brief – *the aim of the day*
3. The rules of brainstorming
4. First Burst
5. Stimulus
   a. The Four R's
   b. Eg. Related World
      i. TV show of cooking – *a related world to gardening*
      ii. List points on a flipchart
      iii. Use those points to come up with ideas, E.g. Get celebrity chefs to write articles on the new gardening website

Repeat using another technique to push the attendees in a new direction.

6. Passionometer, (a fancy name for some stickers). Use stickers – 1 for not so good, 3 for great. It doesn't matter it it's not on brief – the important thing is how people feel about it.

The first thing to do once you've established the rules of an ideas session and discussed the brief, is to have a *First Burst*. A first burst aims to get those really obvious, preconceived ideas out and on paper before moving on. Everyone will come to an ideas session with some pre-conceived ideas of how the project should look. Generally, they are the most obvious ideas and they will have been worked out in some detail. More often than not, they are the safest, less-risky ideas.

Once that is out of the way, and the ideas have been recorded, it's the facilitator's job to begin coaxing the ideas out of the attendees by using stimulus. The Four R's, (which I'll come to), is a very useful tool in steering ideas generation without a session becoming stuck down a certain line of thinking.

The facilitator will use the Idea Brief and insights gathered during the Research Phase as springboards to send the attendees into other areas of thought.

The facilitator will record all the ideas on a single sheet of paper. After the session is finished, the facilitator will go through all of the ideas one by one and the group will rate them by the Passionometer. One sticker for 'not feeling it', and three for 'wow, this is great'.

The most highly rated ideas are shortlisted and then enter the next phase of development.

The Four R's

I mentioned the Four R's as a tool for generating ideas. A facilitator uses them in an ideas session to move the attendees from one idea to the next so they don't begin to analyse or judge previous ideas, or become stale. The Four R's are:

Revolution:

Revolution is turning an idea on its head. Taking assumptions and reversing or removing them. E.g. A pub has four walls and a roof. What if it didn't have walls, but still had a roof?

Re-Expression:

Re-express the idea in a different way or point of view. E.g. What if you were five years old and your parents were buying a booster seat for you. What makes a cool booster seat in your eyes?

Related Worlds:
Think of a related world and use ideas from that world. E.g. Cooking and Gardening. What elements of gardening could be used to sell more recipe books?

Random Links:
Forcing a connection with a random object. E.g. A social networking website and a cactus. Random links often generate ideas which are off brief, but that doesn't matter. Sometimes, the most truly innovative ideas can come with random links. I'm sure Citroén designers were using Random Links when they decided to make the 2CV look like a snail.

Chapter Ten
Putting it together

Case Study for a gardening website

A client has come to you with a proposal to redesign a popular gardening website. The website sells gardening products – everything from plants and tools, to seeds and lawnmowers - a one-stop-shop for every gardener's needs.

You've been tasked with generating ideas for the project and presenting your findings to the client. So, where do you start?

The project team and client team

The first thing to do is establish roles and responsibilities in both the project team and the client team. Ensure you have representatives from most areas of the development process: Design, Client Services, Technical, IA/Usability, and Strategy. If you're part of a small business, then this team could just be you, the client and some of their staff – that's just as good. Remember, the most important thing at this stage is to have everyone's buy-in to the process – it will come in really handy further down the line when you have to present the ideas.

Gathering research

The intial phase of this project is to gather research – not commission it. First of all, try and get your hand on anything related to the project. Spend time consuming the media that the customers of this site will – magazines, tv shows, direct mail and catalogues, packaging and Point of Sale materials – anything that will give you an insight into the gardener's world. This is particularly important for the designer in the team. The other members can gather the materials, but you will begin to make connections and have ideas almost immediately.

Next, you should try and work through any existing quantitive research the client may have to see if you can establish any trends. Look at referrers, user journeys, demographics and segmentation. If the client has any focus group findings, get hold of it, even if it's quite old – it could still have some bearing on the new website ideas.

If you can, interview some gardeners. Get a script prepared with some carefully considered questions. You can use a market research agency to gather together some gardeners, (called a 'sample'). They will ensure the sample accurately represents the target audience of the website.

Now is a good time to audit the existing content of the website. This is the beginnings of an Information Architecture task, but also has relevance to the visual design and branding, and the content ideas of the new site. If it's a redesign, you need to know what you're redesigning.

As this is a gardening site that sells gardening stuff, then the core proposition of the site is to sell products, over the World Wide Web, to its customers. The other stuff on the site is to drive traffic into that process. Currently, this site is just an online catalogue plugged into a payment gateway – it's about selling products. However, the client has indicated that they want to add more value to the website, to retain existing customers, and pull in new customers.

As the website is shifting its focus away from just selling things, then we need to establish 1, What market is it moving into and 2, Who are the competitors in that market.

A competitor audit

A competitor audit is still a data gathering process. You start by examining the competitions brand, product offerings and key messages in the marketplace. What's great about using the World Wide Web for your research is you can actually experience the brands and service of the competitors, rather than just gathering visual material.

A competitor audit can be as detailed as you need it to be to build a complete understanding of the business and its place within the market.

For this website, we've established that there are three main competitors: The BBC Gardening website, The Royal Horticultural Society website, and its biggest commercial rival, Crocus.

Stick it all up

This is where your project starts to resemble a crime case in a classic 70's cop drama. Stick everything you have on a wall. Write down key phrases of research findings, scraps of paper to indicate visual styles, printouts of the competitors website – everything you have so far. Make sure they are just small chunks of information though as these are easier to trend – you don't want reams of paper on the wall.

Step back and try and spot the trends. There may be content trends, visual trends or branding trends. Try and identify some opportunity areas or insights. For this website, we've established the following insights gained from the research.

1. Relationship between gardening and cooking

2. Organic, sustainable gardening

3. Gardening in small spaces

The next step is to write an idea brief for each of these opportunity areas:

1. How do we use the relationship between gardening and cooking to sell more products?

2. How can we influence our customers to be more organic and sustainable?

3. How can our customers buy the right products for their small gardens?

These idea briefs are the springboards to be used in our ideas session.

Idea Development

Gather the team together – the project team and client team if you can – and work through an ideas session using the running order described in the previous chapter. Once you have your ideas recorded, you need to shortlist them. Try and get them down to three ideas for each idea brief. That will give us nine ideas to run with.

Next, we need to refine this list to just three ideas – one for each idea brief; and answer the question they pose. For the sake of this example, we'll use an idea in response to the first idea brief: How do we use the relationship between gardening and cooking to sell more products? The idea we came up with for this was to introduce an editorial element to the website. Have celebrity chefs write articles and endorse gardening products and tools.

To further refine this idea, you can use a great tool for this called AN. A.B.C.

AN stands for **Audience Need.** Who is this idea for? Will they want it, or use it. Ideally, are they crying out for it?

A stands for **Approach.** This is about implementation. How are you going to do it? You really don't need to get completely bogged down in the nitty-gritty of this just yet, but an overall plan would be good at this stage.

B stands for **Benefit.** Why should it be done in the first place? Will there be a competitive advantage? Will you be first to market with this idea?

C stands for **Competition.** What will be your place in the market?

Going through this process should give you a much clearer picture of your idea.

Creative Brief

So, you have your three ideas. They've been dreamt up by the project team and client, so everybody should feel ownership of the ideas. Next, the designer should write a creative brief. This document details the creative requirements for the project. So, for our idea, the creative brief could include:

1. Produce a branded content vehicle for the new celebrity chefs section

2. Document proposed user flow with new content

3. Establish a new design based on the visual research associated with cooking

The important thing to note here is that the creative brief is leading the design team down a road based on the ideas. The ideas were based on insights from the research.

Typography

Typographic design is one of those fields in design that is taken for granted. Many designers just choose a cool font and away they go. Lacking an understanding of the subject as a whole, some see it as the designing of typefaces, whilst others see it as being closely related to the printing industry or print design. Some just see it as fonts. Well, it's all of those things and more.

In 2005, Information Architects, a small web agency in Tokyo, Japan, wrote a couple of articles on their blog. The title seemed to cause quite a stir: '95% of the web is Typography'. It may not come as much of a surprise, but I agree.

Of course, the User–Experience Consultants in the industry will tell you the web is about how users interact with and experience the websites and services they use – it's not just about typography. But what facilitates the experience? Words, mostly. What is the practice of setting and arranging words to convey a message or interface? Typographic design. Information Architects were bang on the money in my view.

Typography is a core building block for brands. Companies such as Microsoft, Audi and the BBC are instantly recognisable, in part due to their typography. This is one of the interesting things about typography on the web. We can't guarantee the fonts that are installed on a user's machine, therefore, we can't rely on bespoke fonts, or specific brand typefaces, in order to convey a brand. This is where a good understanding of the craft of typographic design can make all the difference.

When we first look at typefaces, only the most dramatic differences are apparent. With our lack of experience, we could see the difference between serif and sans–serif, but had no clue which typefaces were good and which weren't. Someone more experienced would come along and completely transform a

3

dull page into a work of clarity and beauty just by changing the typeface. We knew the typeface they'd chosen was better – but why?

Knowing the history of typography, the anatomy of letters, and the classification of typefaces helps us in many ways, even when using the limited fonts supplied by browsers or– with the use of image replacement techniques–thousands of others. Immersing ourselves in typography in design school, and studying these aspects of typefaces, we become keenly aware of even subtle differences between them. We learn to see typefaces in an entirely new light: when the use of each was appropriate; when their features best expressed the intent of the brand, author, or project; and when the use of one face rather than another was an elegant, thoughtful choice, giving a certain 'look' to a page. We learn to stop and think about type.

Chapter Eleven
Anatomy

Typefaces, like most things, are made up
of constituent parts. It is the characteristics
of these parts that gives typefaces their
character.

Q S

t o m y

d g l o v e

Character width

1.	Tail	9.	Stem
2.	Spine	10.	Spur
3.	Apex	11.	Link
4.	Serif	12.	Loop
5.	Bowl	13.	Ear
6.	Finial	14.	Ascender
7.	Counter	15.	Arm
8.	Descender	16.	crossbar

Chapter Twelve
Classification

Typefaces, like other elements of design, such as colour and imagery, communicate. They have defining characteristics that give them personalities.

A good designer will be aware of the different characteristics of typefaces and match those characteristics with the story they are trying to tell. The characteristics of type can be broadly categorised, as we'll see in the following section, based on some of their main design elements.

Serifs

A typeface will have serifs, or it won't. If it doesn't, it's called a sans-serif. If it does, then the serif will either be a bracketed, a hairline, a flare, or a slab serif.

The example shows a bracketed **Serif**

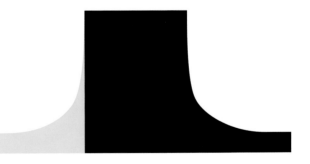

Contrast and whitespace

The relative thickness of the strokes of a typeface determine the amount of whitespace the character has. To introduce more whitespace into a block of text for example, whilst not increasing your leading, you could experiment with using a typeface with less typographic contrast. An example of this would be a typeface that has smaller, or hairline, serifs and wider, more open, counters.

The relative thickness of the strokes of a typeface determine the amount of whitespace the character has.

Minimum contrast   *Extreme contrast*

x–height

The x–height of a typeface is the height of a lowercase 'x'. Different typefaces have different x–heights in relation to their cap–height. X–heights can effect the legibility of typefaces, particularly at a small size. Larger x–heights are more useful for body copy of serif typefaces on the web.

Cap Height

X Height

Baseline

Descender Line

Stress

Stress is the direction of the stroke weight. The more stress, the more acute the angle of the stroke weight. This can give letterforms a more fanciful and intricate appearance.

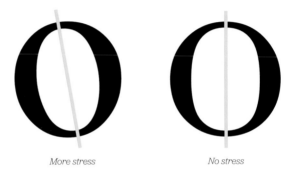

More stress   *No stress*

Weight

Weight is the thickness of the stroke weight. This characteristic is perhaps the one of which people are most aware, such as the use of a bold weight.

Light

Medium

Bold

Black

Classification

Typefaces can be classified into groups based on their different characteristics. Designers have been trying to establish a universally recognised classification system for many years. The most widely accepted one is based on the 1964 classification by the *Deutsche Normenausschuss*. This system classifies typefaces into ten groups.

1. Graphic

The production of typefaces, as we know them, originated in Germany. Gutenberg, of the famous Bible, used movable metal letters instead of the old wooden pieces, and revolutionised printing in the process. Graphic typefaces, based on this Movable Type* system, resemble the local handwriting called Gothic, Blackletter or Textura. This typeface group is the basis for all those terrible heavy metal band logos. Interestingly, the much-maligned Comic Sans belongs to this classification.

Lorem ipsum dolor — Lucida Blackletter

Lorem ipsum dolor — Comic Sans

*Movable Type** is the system of printing and typography using movable pieces of metal type, made by casting from matrices struck by letterpunches.

2. Humanist

Humanist is a type style based on 15th century manuscripts. Humanist is also a sub-category of Lineale.

Centaur

Lorem ipsum dolor

Berkeley Oldstyle

Lorem ipsum dolor

3. Garalde

Modern typeface styles have their roots in Italy. When printing was introduced there, they too wanted to replicate the handwriting of the time. At that time, documents were written in a style called Chancery Italic. Some of the typefaces developed to mimic this style are Garamond, Goudy Old Style and Caslon.

Garamond

Lorem ipsum dolor

Goudy Old Style

Lorem ipsum dolor

At this stage, you can see how two things influenced type design: the local handwriting style and preference, and the sophistication of the printing process. Gradually, those two drifted apart as the materials for printing, (the presses, paper and ink), allowed for more stylised type designs to be developed.

4. Transitional

Transitional typefaces are lighter in appearance than Garalde. The serifs are more horizontal, and the emphasis is vertical rather than slanted. John Baskerville designed possibly the most well-known, named after himself, in the mid 18th century.

Lorem ipsum dolor

Baskerville

Lorem ipsum dolor

Georgia

5. Didone

Didone is home to elegant type with highly contrasting strokes and hairline serifs. Bodini is perhaps the typeface that exemplifies this group.

Lorem ipsum dolor

Bodini

Lorem ipsum dolor

Didot

6. Slab Serif

As technology advanced, so the type designs changed. The Industrial Revolution brought with it the introduction of mechanical typesetting. It also fueled an advertising market that demanded strong and powerful typefaces to sell products. Slab Serif, or Egyptian, type designs were born. A good example of a classic is Rockwell. A more contemporary version would be the typeface for the new Guardian newspaper redesign in the UK.

Jubilat

Lorem ipsum dolor

Rockwell

Lorem ipsum dolor

7. Lineale

This is the classification for sans-serif typefaces. Originally designed for posters and headlines, sans-serif typefaces quickly became standard fare for printing. This group is divided into four subcategories: Grotesque, Neo-grotesque, Geometric, and Humanist.

Franklin Gothic Book

Lorem ipsum dolor

News Gothic MT

Lorem ipsum dolor

8. Glyphic

This categorisation has been the centre of some debate over the years. Glyphic is supposed to be the classification of stone-carved forms, rather than handwritten forms. However, stone-carved forms are based on hand-painted letter forms, (it's where serifs are widely regarded as originating from).

LOREM IPSUM DOLOR

Trajan Pro

Lorem ipsum dolor

Optima

9. Script

Script type designs emulate ornate, swishing handwriting.

Lorem ipsum dolor

Zapfino

Lorem ipsum dolor

Brush Script MT

10. Stylised

Stylised type designs are one large classification for all those weird and sometimes wonderful typefaces that have become available since the advent of cheap computers and programs which allow anyone with a bit of skill and an idea to create and distribute a typeface.

Mido

Lorem ipsum dolor

Fontin Sans

Lorem ipsum dolor

Iconic typefaces

At certain times, typefaces can come to represent a specific era. It takes a collection of designers or typographers to suddenly start using a particular typeface in influential publications for the snowball to slowly start gathering momentum. Before you know it, the most unlikely of fashionable typefaces crop up in unfashionable places.

Poor Template Gothic

As a young designer in the 1990's, I was reading all the publications everyone else was: Emigré, Raygun, Eye, The Face, etc. During this time, Emigré was very popular amongst my industry peers. They produced and commissioned typefaces as well. One proved to be so popular in the 1990's it was a victim of its own success and was overused. As a result, I don't think I've seen it used by graphic designers in the last ten years. The typeface was Template Gothic, designed by Barry Deck.

The first time I saw Template Gothic in use, (rather than only being displayed in Emigré), was in the mid-nineties in Raygun magazine. Raygun was the music magazine piloted by every designer's hero of the time, David Carson. If David Carson thought this typeface was cool, then of course, we did too. Every designer across the globe began to set headlines in Template Gothic. Then, the fashion spread from editorial design to advertising and finally, packaging. It was at this point, as had happened to Helvetica Light/ Thin in the early nineties, every designer stopped using it–except the bad ones, of course. Template Gothic was then shunned by most designers, as it was used in the most inappropriate places–a real shame.

Lorem ipsum dolor

Template Gothic

What makes a classic?

A classic typeface is like a classic suit: durable. It can be used to convey multiple messages on varying media over decades– sometimes centuries. It survives fads, it's versatile, and it's so well designed that designers from different eras or with different tastes respect it.

Other examples of classic or iconic typefaces

VAG Rounded

VAG Rounded was commissioned by Volkswagen and Audi Group, (hence the name). Similar in many ways to Helvetica Rounded, VAG Rounded has a youthful, playful feel and has been widely used for all manner of applications - from refrigerator magnets to children's toys.

Lorem ipsum dolor

VAG Rounded

Meta

Like most typefaces, Meta was designed for a specific purpose.
It was designed by Erik Spiekermann as the corporate font for
the Deutsche Bundespost, the German equivalent of the Post
Office. Like Helvetica, Meta has been widely used as a corporate
typeface. It has a somewhat soulless character, (though not as
much as Helvetica), which makes it easy to adopt as a corporate
typeface– it's safe, clean, and modern.

Meta
Lorem ipsum dolor

Mrs. Eaves

Mrs. Eaves is actually a redraw of another classic, Baskerville, by
type designer Zuzana Licko, of Emigré font foundry. Its elegant
italics and ligature weight captured designers' imaginations in
the late 1990's. Emigré released a very useful little application
with this font that made setting type with the extensive ligature
characters, (which we'll discuss later), as simple as copying and
pasting – years before widespread Open Type adoption.

Mrs. Eaves
Lorem ipsum dolor

Chapter Thirteen
Hierarchy

Typographic hierarchy

Typographic hierarchy, put simply, is how different faces, weights and sizes of typefaces structure a document. It may do this by separating sections, by indicating the degree of importance of each piece of information or by making the organisation of the document immediately apparent to the reader. Some of these hierarchical devices are well–established conventions, such as cross heads and folios.

To keep it simple I'm going to concentrate on two things: size and weight.

Early typographers usually created their manuscripts using one font, one size, and one colour, interspersed with hand–painted illuminations. The product of such typographers gives a flat quality to the information, almost mesmeric.

Take a look at some early manuscripts and the letters themselves–especially the older Blackletter styles– appear similar. M's look like u's, y's look like p's and so on. As beautiful as these manuscripts are, other than the illuminations, they are devoid of structure within the content. There is no typographic hierarchy.

Evolution of the scale

In the Sixteenth Century, European typographers developed a series of typeface sizes, a scale, (the musical analogy is a good one – stick with me). As shown in the diagram, they are sizes we're all familiar with. Six point through seventy–two point type has remained pretty much intact for over four hundred years. In fact, they are the default font sizes in many applications, (give or take a few).

So, what's so special about these sizes? Well, because this scale of sizes has been used for centuries, and the size of each point in the scale relates in a specific ratio to the size of the others, if set correctly type in this scale will appear more pleasing to the eye. An interesting point: originally the sizes in the scale were referred to by name instead of by point size.

a a a a a a a a a a a a a a
6 7 8 9 10 11 12 14 18 21 24 36 48 60 72

Here are a few examples of some of the older names:

6pt: *nonpareil*

7pt: *minion*

8pt: *brevier or small text*

9pt: *bourgeois or galliard*

10pt: *long primer or garamond*

11pt: *small pica or philosophy*

12pt: *pica*

14pt: *english or augustin*

18pt: *great primer*

21pt: *double small pica or double pica*

24pt: *double pica or two-line pica*

36pt: *double great primer or 2-line great primer*

New software and modern methods of typesetting, have allowed character heights that fall outside of, and within, this scale. This freedom has resulted in a typographic free-for-all, allowing designers to pick sizes that may not be related to one another as they are with this scale. Is this a bad thing? I'd argue that it is.

Let's go back to the music analogy. It's like composing a discordant piece of music: clashing notes, clashing type. If it's clashing you're after, that's fine. If, however, you're after harmony and melody that stands the hairs up on the back of your neck, stick to the notes in the scale, folks!

Application of the scale

So let's put some of this into practice. I'm going to use my design studio's website, *markboultondesign.com*, as an example.

I started off designing this website with something very specific in mind – strong typography. I wanted to make sure this site would work based on a simple, clear hierarchy of typography set against a simple modular grid, with plenty of white space on which to 'hang' a number of design elements, (the company's work, for example).

Following the typographic scale described in the previous section, I set about applying this to the CSS-based design.

These are the elements for the typographic hierarchy. Note, I'm using pixels as my base measurement, not points. And, yes, I do know the pixels are different on different platforms, (for example, Mac versus Windows).

The thing about type sizes in CSS is that if you want to remain true to typographic tradition, you must specify ems or percentages based on an absolute unit of measurement – in this case a pixel. If you use the relative – small, x–small etc. – there aren't enough declarations to complete the scale, and the sizing of each increment is fixed at 1.5 going up the scale or 0.66% going down, (apparently this depends and was also changed to somewhere between 1.0 and 1.2 in CSS2). Anyway, I don't want to get fixated on the best CSS approach to this. This chapter is about typography, not CSS.

These are the pixel sizes for my main headings:

11px / 16.5px – *Body copy and leading.*
24px – *Main heading used as section headings on the home page, portfolio home page and entries.*
18px – *Headings for journal entries and portfolio subheadings.*
16px – *All navigational and content tertiary headings.*
13px – *All other headed elements.*

This would give me the following styles visually:

H1 – Section Headings
H2 – Entries Headings
H3 – Navigation Headings
H4 – All other headed elements

Body copy and leading

These translate in the following way in CSS, using percentages for scaling purposes, basing the scaling from an 11px base size.

11px / 1.5em – *Body copy and leading.*
218% – *Main heading used as section headings on the home page, portfolio home page and entries.*
164% – *Headings for journal entries and portfolio subheadings.*
145% – *All navigational and content tertiary headings.*
118% – *All other headed elements.*

So, within my CSS file, it looks like this:

```
body {
        font: 11px/1.5em "Georgia";
}

h1, h2, h3, h4, h5, h6 {
        font-family: georgia, times, sans-serif;

        font-weight: normal;
}

h1 {
        font-size: 218%;
}

h2 {
        font-size: 164%;
}

h3 {
        font-size: 145%;
}

h4 {
        font-size: 118%;
}
```

Using these values for the size of the headings creates a natural relationship between them. The typography is harmonious as a result and it only took about five minutes to implement.

Size really does matter

It really does. If you take anything away from this chapter, please let it be this: Stop and think about your type sizes, just for five minutes. Plan them; don't just choose whatever you feel like from the dropdown in Photoshop. Make sure they are 'in tune' and then apply the theory to whatever medium and content you are designing for.

Style and weight

Typeface weights are the different styles within a typeface family.
It can be confusing, as the term 'weight' does not mean 'more bold',
or 'heavier'. Many typefaces have a core set of weights: Roman,
(normal weight), Italic, Bold, Bold Italic and Small caps. There are
many variations to this, and many typefaces have a huge range of
weights, from Thin, through to Extra Bold, from Ornamentals
to Ligatures.

Typeface weight, and the choice of weight, is perhaps one
area of typography that to most designers is simply a matter of
choice–they are presented with an entire family of weights within
a typeface to choose from.

That choice is often dictated by answering a design problem
that is aesthetically or content–motivated. Maybe a designer wants
to set some headlines in ALL CAPS just for some variation; all he
has to do is choose that weight from a dropdown or to define it in
their CSS. What many designers do not realise is that there are
rules which should govern the choice of weight, (a typographic
pecking order), which when followed, aid the designer's
typesetting and can produce stunning results.

Solving the design problem

Let's start by addressing the root of the decision to set type in
different weights to solve a design problem. I mentioned that this
problem stems from two main concerns:

- An aesthetic problem. *The designer sets type in a certain
  weight to add style or solve some kind of visual or
  compositional issue.*

- A content problem. *The designer needs to set a different
  weight because the content dictates it. The main reasons are
  that the language of the content may dictate special
  typographic treatment, the tone of voice may be different,
  it may be a quote, or it may be a structural device such as an
  unordered list.*

There may be other reasons as well, but I believe these are the
main cause.

Here you can see some of the weights set out and joined by lines. The red lines represent the core typeface family. Some typographers would argue that without these core weights, typefaces are reduced to being used for titles only. I'll leave that one open for debate!

The other lines show how designers can move along the lines when setting type.

For example, if a designer has set type in roman and they need to add emphasis to a certain point in the copy, they would follow the lines to any on the second lines – bold lower case, small caps, full caps, and italic lower case or sloped small caps. If they were to jump to, say, bold italic lower case, or a more extreme example, bold sloped caps, the effect would be horrible.

If the designer is setting type in bold lower case they could go on to add bold caps, or bold italic lower case without much bother. You get the idea?

So, following this simple roadmap can ensure that your typography adheres to some simple hierarchical rules and as a result your typography will take on a harmonious feel. Don't just take my word for it though, set some type, use the rules and you'll see.

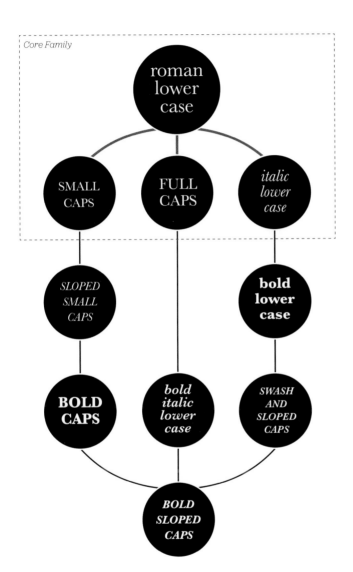

First a bit of history

Uppercase and lowercase, and the relationship between them, have been around for over twelve hundred years. Small caps, ornamentals and Arabic figures were early additions to the roman.

Italics were a strange bunch to begin with. They didn't associate themselves with lower case roman, as we usually see today, but with roman caps and small caps. It's only in recent times that usage of italic, within roman, was deemed to be typographically correct. Some of the newest additions to the weights of typefaces came with bold, and condensed, as late as the early nineteenth century. These were generally used in place of italics and small caps. Bold typefaces have now become a standard way of differentiating in typesetting, particularly on screen where italics are a little more difficult to read.

A type family with all of these weights forms a balanced series that is not only historically accurate but creates harmonious typography. If the setting of copy was reversed, so italics were used as body copy, Caps was used as pull-quotes and bold was used as access structure, (folios, running heads etc), not only would the body of text look terrible, it would also be very difficult to read.

Primary	roman lower case
Secondary	Roman Upper Case ROMAN SMALL CAPS *italic lower case*
Tertiary	*True Italic (Cursive) Upper Case* *SLOPED SMALL CAPS* **bold lower case**
Quaternary	*False Italic (Sloped Roman) Upper Case* **Bold Upper Case** **BOLD SMALL CAPS** ***bold italic lower case***
Quintary	***Bold Italic (Sloped Roman) Upper Case***

Chapter Fourteen
Typesetting

Typographic design is such a large topic in the practice of design that some of the constituent parts need a bit of individual attention.

Take type design, for example. The font industry is big business, and rightly so, but to many people this is what typography is, simply choosing a font. That's it. 'My typography is done, move on to the colours.' Hang on one minute; you've forgotten typesetting.

Typesetting, as defined by Dictionary.com, is:

> 'To set (written material) into type; compose.'

Not very enlightening, but the word 'compose', used in this context is an important word. 'Composition'– amongst the many definitions relating it to typesetting, I like this one:

> 'Arrangement of artistic parts so as to form a unified whole.'

Typesetting has a rich history in the craft of the printing trade where compositors worked, by hand and later by machines, to produce printed material. Then, along came desktop publishing and things changed. The basic principles, (I'll get onto some of them), remained the same, but something was lost in translation. Typesetting was no longer being done by skilled tradesmen, (compositors), but by graphic designers, who arguably didn't have the skills, but were cheap because they worked on labour–saving computers. So, from the late 1980s onwards, typesetting suffered and, as a result, typography suffered.

    This may be a little melodramatic for the print–based world, but things are a whole lot worse on the web. True, there are technical constraints relating to which font you can have, but as I said, there's more to typography than the font.

The measure

The 'measure' is the name given to the width of a body of type.
There are several units of measurement used for defining the
measure's width. The three basic units are:

- One point = 1/72 of an inch
- One pica = 12 points
- One em = The distance horizontally equal to the type size, in
  points, that you are using, e.g., 1em of 12pt type is 12pt.

But, with the advent of DTP packages and website design the
following are also now used:

- Millimetres = mm
- Pixels = px
- X-height = ex

There is a measurement of ex in CSS which relates to the x-height
of a character, (at least it's supposed to), but in reality it's half an
em. The x-height isn't embedded information in most fonts, so the
browser just interprets it in terms of ems. Interestingly, this is one
thing that IE5 on a Mac did well; it internally renders a lower case
x, of the font you are using, and then counts the number of pixels.

There is an optimum width for a measure, for legibility, and that
is defined by the number of characters in the lines on a page. A
general good rule of thumb is two to three alphabets in length, or
52 – 78 characters, (including spaces). Keep your measure within
these guidelines and you should have no problem with legibility.
Please note that this figure will vary widely with research; this is
just the figure I use and it seems to work well as a general rule
of thumb.

CSS and fluid layouts?

How does a measure react to the increase and decrease in size
of the body of text in a fluid layout? The entire grid would have
to adapt to these CSS-defined changes. This is an interesting
discussion point and challenge. While staying true to the
philosophy of the fluidity of web design, the designer must still
make readability a priority.

The measure and leading.

A fundamental rule is that your leading should be wider than your word spacing. This is because when the balance between them is correct, your eye will move along the line instead of down the lines.

If your measure is wider than the guidelines for optimum legibility, then increase the leading – or 'line-height' as it's sometimes called. This will have the effect of increasing legibility. Your leading should increase proportionally to your measure. Small measure, less leading. Wide measure, more leading. It's a simple but effective rule.

Reversing out?

When reversing colour out, e.g., white text on black, make sure you increase the leading and tracking, and decrease your font-weight. This applies to all widths of measure. White text on a black background is a higher contrast than black on white, so the letterforms need to be wider apart, lighter in weight and have more space between the lines.

Tracking

The general rule of thumb in tracking your words, (not the characters), is that the shorter the line length, the tighter the tracking should be, and longer line lengths call for looser tracking.

The big pink bus, was big, pink and most importantly, a bus.

Your responsibility

Following these simple rules will ensure your bodies of text will be as legible as they can be. These rules come from a typographic craft background and unfortunately, for our industry in particular, they aren't being taught as much as they should be in the art schools around the world. As a result, they aren't being practiced and correct, well-considered typography is taking a nose-dive.

It's our responsibility, as designers, to embrace the rules that were born of a craft that goes back hundreds of years.

Leading

Leading, or line-height, is the distance between lines of text. The term comes from a time when blocks of letters were spaced by adding lead strips. The more strips that were added, the more the leading.

For most applications, you should add a little more leading than you think necessary. For 9pt type, I always set my leading at 13pt, which is right at the supposed tolerance level for legibility.

Type can be aligned to the leading values in a document – this is called a 'baseline grid' as shown below.

The big pink bus, was big, pink and most importantly, a bus.

Leading can also have fractional values of this baseline grid, which is called 'incremental leading'. For example, if a document has type set 9pt on 13pt, the baseline grid is 13pt. If there is a caption, where the type is smaller than the main body – say 7pt – then it would be odd if this was aligned to the main baseline grid because the leading would be too great. With Incremental leading, the leading of the caption has a fraction of the baseline grid value.

As shown on the diagram below, the caption type (a) aligns with every fifth line of the main body of text (b). The result is a relationship between the two, that if an arbitrary leading were chosen, wouldn't exist previously.

Lorem ipsum .... Lorem ipsum dolor **b**
dolor sit amet, ... sit amet, consectetur
consectetur .... adipiscing elit.
adipiscing elit. .... Vestibulum mattis nisi
Vestibulum .... **a**

The right glyph for the job

One of the aspects of typesetting which seems to be lacking in the design profession – and I'm as guilty of this as the next designer–is that of a thorough understanding of the written word, and a good grasp of punctuation, grammar and structure. Good typesetters should really know the language in which they are composing.

A glyph is the visual representation of a character in a font. Sometimes, glyphs can represent one character or a few, (depending on the language). Using the right glyph in the right place is vitally important for good typesetting. Sometimes, this responsibility falls squarely on the author's shoulders, particularly for punctuation, but more often than not, it's a joint responsibility between author, editor and typesetter.

The ellipsis

An ellipsis is a punctuation mark comprised of a series of dots, or points (...) indicating an omission in the text, an interruption or hesitation. The ellipsis is usually three dots, although there are instances when it appears to be four. Here are some guidelines for using ellipses properly:

Most fonts have a built-in ellipsis character, so you can use the following to insert an ellipsis:

- Mac: Option-semicolon
- Windows: `ALT 0133`
- XHTML entity: `&hellip;`
- Character reference: `&#8230;`
- Unicode reference: `u2026`

There are a few grammatical/typographic rules to follow:

1. An ellipsis at the end of a sentence is not followed by a full-stop (period) unless it's inside a quote or the following sentence is functionally complete, e.g., I thought 'we could go...'.

2. When a complete sentence is ended in an ellipsis, indicating some omitted material, there is a full-stop and the next sentence begins with a capital letter, e.g. Well, I thought... Never mind, it doesn't matter.

3. Sentences ending in an exclamation, or question mark retain their mark after the ellipsis, e.g., Could we...?

Quotation marks

Quotation marks, also called 'inverted commas', are used to wrap quotations. In the UK, it is common practice to use single marks (") except for when there are quotes within quotes, where double marks are used. In the US it is common practice to use double marks (""). Again, the proper methods of inserting these marks should be used:

Single marks:
- Mac: `Option+]` for left, `Shift+Option+]` for right
- PC: `ALT 0145` for left, `ALT 0146` for right
- XHTML entity: `&lsquo;` for left, `&rsquo;` for right
- Character reference:`&#0145` for left, `&#0146` for right
- Unicode reference:`&#8216` for left, `&#8217` for right

Double marks:
- Mac: `Option+[` for left, `Shift+Option+[` for right
- PC: `ALT 0147` for left, `ALT 0148` for right
- XHTML entity: `&ldquo;` for left, `&rdquo;` for right
- Character reference:`&#0147` for left, `&#0148` for right
- Unicode reference:`&#8220;` for left, `&#8221;` for right

Quotation marks are the poor fellows who have perhaps suffered the most at the hands of computing and desktop publishing. The marks on your keyboard next to the colon and semi colon are not quotation marks, they are primes and double-primes. A prime is the symbol commonly used for feet (12'), a double prime for inches (12' 6"). Primes can be slanted and can therefore sometimes look like quotation marks, so care needs to be taken to make sure you use the right glyph. Some typefaces have so-called neutral quotes. They look a bit like primes, but are in fact quotation marks without the slant – a relic from the typewriter age.

Ligatures

fi fi *fi fi*

Ligatures are combinations of letters–some of them are functional, some are decorative. They are more commonly seen in serif faces, although ligatures in sans-serif faces–such as Gill Sans and Scala Sans–are important to the typeface and should be used.

They are generally comprised of certain characters that are created to stop collision of elements of letterforms. Take the letter 'f' of a serif typeface. In lower case, especially italic, the top and tail of the f move into the character space next to it. These overlaps are what typographers call kerns.

It's when these overlaps collide with letters next to them that we have problems. Take lower case 'f' and lower case 'i', probably the most widely used ligature. When set in Roman, the ascender of the 'f' collides with the dot of the 'i'; the effect is much worse when set in italic. Type designers therefore combined the character into the 'fi' ligature. As you can see, the dot from the 'i' is simply removed.

fi fl ff ffl ft

Examples of Ligatures

Ligatures and language have been closely tied throughout typographic history. Typographers in the sixteenth century devised ligatures to cope with common occurrences of letters in latin – fi, fl, ff, ffl, ft (shown above). You will find at least a couple of these in most fonts. But, as language has changed to incorporate different words, especially English, the need for more obscure ligatures has grown.

Take the word fjord for example. The ascender of the 'f' will collide with the dot of the lower case 'j'. This is resolved the same way as the fi ligature in that the dot is removed from the 'j'. The trouble with less common ligatures like this is that they generally aren't in the standard character set of a font, so we kind of have to make do, or if setting type in a program like Adobe Illustrator, make them by hand. And this brings me neatly onto practical usage of ligatures.

Usage in print

I tend to use ligatures specifically for headlines. Occasionally, if the job demands it, I will use ligatures for body copy as well, but this does tend to make typesetting a little time– consuming.

If, for example, I'm creating a logotype for a coffee shop called 'Flow's Fine Beans', (a convenient amount of ligatures present there!), the name could simply be set in a font that does not require ligatures, but this could make the logotype quite plain. The font chosen could be serif, which might include ligatures, but special care must be given to the kerning and overall appearance when setting logotypes that use ligatures.

flow's *fine beans*

flow's *fine beans*

This logotype, shown above, is typed using Mrs. Eaves. See how the ligatures appear too close to each other creating dense areas of type? The gaps between certain letterforms are also unsettling to the eye. This needs to be manually kerned.

If the type is set carefully, the ligatures add typographic interest to the words. They add character and begin to tell a story about Flow's shop – it's a classy place with nice coffee too!

Careful attention to detail at this stage can help define a logotype and go a long way to help define brand message – all through the simple use of ligatures.

But what about on the web?

Ligatures are in the hands of the fonts and the browsers. As with all web design, there are inconsistencies between the two, so use them wisely. Also, screen readers are bound to have a hard time with ligatures, as will Google. Like a lot of web design, until the technology catches up, we may have to leave them out.

Dashes

The hyphen

72pt.

Hyphen

The hyphen, or the 'hyphen–minus', is what you get when you press the key next to zero on the standard qwerty keyboard- well mine anyway, (for all those pedants out there). It's the shortest of the three types of dashes and is often used incorrectly. I'll look at the most common correct uses of the hyphen first, before moving on to the dashes it is often used, incorrectly, to replace.

There are two types of hyphen: the 'soft' hyphen and the 'hard' hyphen. Sometimes they are different lengths, but this depends on the typeface.

Hard hyphen

The hard hyphen joins two words together wherever they are positioned on the same line. For example, 'run–of–the–mill'. It's set closed up, (which means no space either side).

Soft hyphen

The soft hyphen indicates where a word has been split at the end of a line. Arguably, there's very little use for the soft hyphen on the web when the user has so much control over the presentation of the type.

There are many grammatical rules associated with hyphens, which differ greatly from language to language. For British typesetting, and the English language, I'd recommend getting yourself a copy of the Oxford Guide to Style, (the old Hart's Typesetter's Rules).

The en dash

72pt.
En dash

The en dash is one en in length. It's slightly longer than a hyphen and half the width of an em dash. Em and en are typographic measures based on point size. An em is equal to the size of the set type (E.g. 12pt) and an en is half that.

1. An en dash is used, closed up, (meaning, without spaces on either side), in-between elements that show a range, e.g, Monday–Sunday, 1985–2005. It is also used when the end element is not known: Joe Bloggs (1984–)*.

2. The en dash can be used to show the meaning of to and from, e.g., on–off switch.

3. The en dash can also be used to join compound adjectives that include multiple words or hyphens already. In this case the en dash clarifies what is grouped with what, for example, high-priority–high-pressure tasks.

4. In Unicode, the en dash is U+2013 (decimal 8211). In HTML, the numeric forms are – and –. The HTML entity is –.

---

* It's common practice in North American typesetting to use an em dash for this purpose.

The em dash

72pt.

Em dash

The em dash, as its name suggests, is one em in width. The em dash has been neglected by many writers and designers over recent years. Frequently replaced by the hyphen, or that relic from typewriter days, the double hyphen (--)*, I think it's about time we gave this little fella the time of day.

Once again, there are differing grammatical usages depending on the language being used, and the country in which the text is written. In British and North American typesetting there are a few simple rules:

1. Use the em dash closed up in written dialogue to indicate an interruption, for example, 'What a load of–', but his words were lost on her.

2. It can also be used to indicate an interruption in thought within a sentence, when a comma would be too weak to separate the thought from the rest of the sentence, and a period would be too strong. This might happen at the end of a sentence or it can be used either side of an interruption–like this one–and is set closed up.

3. In Unicode, the em dash is U+2014 (decimal 8212). In HTML, the numeric forms are — and —. The HTML entity is —.

It's worth noting that em dash usage is inconsistent, not only across languages, but also across house styles. The most common replacements are an en dash and the hyphen, both set with a space, (or a hair space), either side.

* The usage of this is of course valid on a typewriter where, as with most monospaced fonts, the hyphens, em and en dashes all are similar length.

Lists and hanging punctuation

Hanging punctuation, too, has suffered at the hands of certain software products. The term refers to glyph positioning that creates the illusion of a uniform edge of text.

It's most commonly used for pull-quotes, but I feel the most neglected use is that of bulleted lists.

With the advent of desktop publishing it suddenly became very easy and cost-effective to produce bodies of text.

The problem was these bodies of text work within a box. Every character in this box had to be within the box – hanging punctuation requires characters, such as a quotation mark at the beginning of a quote, to be outside of the box.

This was a problem for the software and as a result was ignored.

An important aspect of typesetting was just swept under the carpet like that. It's a great shame.

Things are now improving: Adobe Indesign is offering support for hanging punctuation, and the latest version of Quark may, too. Not sure about Microsoft Word – probably not.

Lists

Without hanging bullets

Lorem ipsum dolor sit amet.
· Duis tempus dui nec dui.
· Curabitur sapien nibh, ullamcorper sed,
  convallis id, tincidunt eget, sem.
· Pellentesque habitant morbi tristique
senectus et netus et malesuada fames ac.

Ranged-left body of type is pretty much destroyed, aesthetically, when punctuation isn't hung. The eye looks for straight lines everywhere, and when type is indented in this way, it destroys the flow of text.

Lorem ipsum dolor sit amet.
· Duis tempus dui nec dui.
· Curabitur sapien nibh, ullamcorper sed,
convallis id, tincidunt eget, sem.
· Pellentesque habitant morbi tristique
senectus et netus et malesuada fames ac.

With hanging punctuation, the flow of text on the left side is uninterrupted. The bullets, glyphs or numbers sit in the gutter thus highlighting and unifying the list itself. This representation of a list is more visually sophisticated and more legible.

Pull–quotes

Without hanging punctuation

Lorem ipsum dolor sit amet.

" Curabitur sapien nibh, ullamcorper sed, convallis id, tincidunt eget, morbi."

Pellentesque habitant morbi tristique senectus et netus et malesuada fames ac.

Nothing is more irritating than badly typeset quotes. The interruption of the flow is considerable and the overall effect is unsightly.

Lorem ipsum dolor sit amet.

" Curabitur sapien nibh, ullamcorper sed, convallis id, tincidunt eget, morbi. "

Pellentesque habitant morbi tristique senectus et netus et malesuada fames ac.

Quotation marks should be 'hung' as you see in the diagram above. In this example, the quotation marks are hung either side of the quote. Once again, this allows uninterrupted reading for the audience.

Tables and forms

Tables of data and forms should be given careful design consideration. If you forget the usability factors associated with forms on the World Wide Web for just one moment, the actual visual design of tables and forms should be quite simple: Use space well and make sure things line up. Well, it's not always that easy.

I had a baptism of fire with forms and tables. When I was 21, I had a summer internship at an advertising agency in Manchester, UK. In addition to the usual lowly tasks of being the 'Spraymount Boy' – yes, for a while there, I virtually lived in the cutting room – I was tasked with helping one of the artworkers, (unfortunately, not my best mate who got me the job, but a rather grumpy little man from Warrington), to help set the tables and forms for a huge plumbing catalogue.

This thing was enormous – close to a thousand pages of cutouts, tables and order forms. The grid was set, the type styles were signed off, and it was just left to me and this bloke to fill the pages with thousands upon thousands of little nuts, bolts, thingemies and whatsits. Next to each cutout was a table that referred to the item's specifications, which, in turn, related to an enormous order form in the back of the catalogue. Yes, this was in the days of mail order – way back in 1994.

As tedious as that particular project was, it taught me some valuable lessons for setting tables and forms. Here are some of them:

1. Use a thick rule to denote headlines and thin rules to separate lines.

2. Don't use alternate background colours in rows, just use one and white.

3. If you can, don't use vertical lines. Let the data in the tables indicate the columns.

4. To give emphasis to a column heading, set it in CAPS.

5. To emphasise a column, set it in bold, or highlight with a different background colour.

6. Range numerical data right.

7. Give more padding to the bottom of items than to the top. You can still keep the same overall line-height, but this gives the reader a sense of more whitespace.

	AW	AW	AW	AW	AW	AW ❹
Pontypridd d	--	--	0519	--	--	--
Trefforest d	--	--	0521	--	--	--
Cathays d	--	--	0539	--	--	--
Caerffili/Caerphilly d	--	--	--	--	0600	-- ❼
Heol y Frenhines/Cardiff Queen Street d	--	--	0544	--	0615	--
Caerdydd Canolog/Cardiff Central d	0515	0542	0550	0607	0625 ❸	0645
Grangetown d	0519	0546	0554	0611	0629	0649
Heol Dingle/Dingle Road d	--	--	--	--	--	0653
Penarth a	--	--	--	--	--	0657
Cogan d ❺	0522	0549	0557	0614	0632	--
Eastbrook d	0525	0552	0600	0617	0635	--
Dinas Powys d	0527	0554	0602	0619	0637 ❻	--
Tregatwg/Cadoxton d	0531	0558	0606	0623	0641	--
Dociau'r Barri/Barry Dock d	0533	0600	0608	0625	0643	--
Y Barri/Barry d	0537	0604	0612	0629	0647	--
Ynys y Barri/Barry Island a	0542	0609	--	0634	0652	--
Rhoose d	--	--	0618	--	--	--
Llantwit Major d	--	--	0629	--	--	--
Bridgend a	--	--	0642	--	--	--

(Callout markers ❶ and ❷ appear at the top rule and near Caerdydd Canolog/Cardiff Central d respectively.)

Chapter Fifteen
Printing the Web

The screen is just one of the media types for which we have to design. Another media type, which I feel is often neglected during the design process for a website, is print.

There are times when a web designer has to know about print design—not just the values and aesthetics of designing for print, but the terminology, measurements and production values that are important in print, including typesetting.

Print alternatives to web pages have been around for a while; we've all seen them, in one form or another. Usually, they are associated with a 'print version' button, which upon clicking, renders the page without any navigation and, if you're lucky, increases the font size. This is generally about it. Many sites offer this functionality but I have to question whether, due to time constraints, users click this button, or if like me, they just print the page straight from their browser.

In which case they will get something like this, (prints from Guardian Unlimited and The Times).

The Times Online
www.timesonline.co.uk

The Guardian
www.guardian.co.uk

There is a way, other than 'print only' versions, of rendering this content for a printer. I'm referring to print style sheets, or, more specifically, a CSS file, which has been authored for print media and declared as 'print' in the 'media' attribute of the link tag.

The last to be thought about

It's been my experience over the past few years that, despite a very clear need for users to print out web pages, designers very rarely address this need. Why is that? Do we think that print is important in a screen-based environment? Jason Santa Maria, graphic designer, had this to say when I asked about it recently:

> 'Many people still see the web as a temporary medium, one that is always changing and where content is potentially irretrievable. I know many people who love to print things they find on sites, from articles to recipes to photos, to view when they are away from the computer or for their own personal archive. There's no reason that information shouldn't either support your brand or be designed with the same care as your site.'·

Khoi Vinh, Design Director of NYTimes.com and the popular weblog, Subtraction.com, agreed with Jason:

> 'Having developed web solutions for many text-heavy publications in my career, at least one user scenario remains: people like to print long passages of screen-based text for reading offline.'

This then begs the question: If printing from the web is so important for users, then why do we see print-based templates either being left to the last minute, or being developed by technical teams, rather than designers? In addition to implementation though, what else influences the decision for offering a print alternative? Khoi makes some valid points about revenue generation, through advertising, in the print versions:

> 'Designers are focused on the immediate, knowable and sharable result of what gets rendered on the screen, so it's natural to consider print media stylesheets an afterthought. But other factors contribute to this, too, notably the monetization of 'printer friendly' versions of articles at many publication sites.

That is, rather than offer a print-based set of CSS rules, many sites will offer an alternative screen rendering of the same article, slimmed down to just the primary text– we've all seen this. Very often, those print-friendly views are sold to advertisers for sponsorship, so in those cases at least, there's a financial reason not to create a print media style sheet.'

This is something that I hadn't really considered when researching this book. Jason also raised some interesting points about the medium:

'Because print stylesheets are perceived as somewhat non– essential to most site creators, their main focus is their website and the appearance of it in various browsers. I think many people see print as a secondary medium, like mobile phones, that is optional. And I suppose it is a secondary medium, as far as the web is concerned, but there is very little preparation involved in producing some simple styles for print.'

Perhaps designers assume that because print styles are deemed secondary that they can be added at a later date.

This can, at times, be true, but developing the example for this book, I found that creating a print style called for revisiting the code in the template to make sure the content flow was correct and that design elements could be added. So, in that sense, I'm not sure that assumption is true.

* Extracted from blog post *http://www.markboulton.co.uk/journal/comments/five_simple_steps_to_typesetting_on_the_web_printing_the_web/*

Now that I've given you some context, I'll get into the actual design of the printed page.

Printing the web: The Guardian

For a good example, I looked for a text-heavy site, with a strong on and offline brand that could benefit from print styles. I chose the British newspaper, The Guardian.

Why? Well, The Guardian has an established website. The paper version was recently redesigned and now there is somewhat of a gap between the appearance of the website and printed material. The first task was to design what the printed page from the website would look like.

Design the printed page

I feel the process of designing the printed content of a website is as important as designing for other media: screen readers, mobile and small screen. The design process is the same as designing for any other media. You have to understand the context, the production and the delivery.

Luckily I chose an example with a very strong offline design from which to draw inspiration. I began by researching The Guardian's redesign and analysing its components: the grid, typography, colour and composition.

I chose a typical page layout, which included running heads, article headline, date, author, noting all the content that would go into the online version.

It was clear from this example which areas of the design I would need to replicate to ensure a quality reproduction for the print styles. I then began to shape up the design.

Shaping the page

I begin most design tasks by drawing thumbnails. This one was no different.

As you can see, I knew there were some important issues I wanted to address even at this early stage. Width of the measure is an essential consideration for printing on an average desktop printer. I opted for a full-width measure. Although this may hinder legibility due to the long line length, I feel this is acceptable, considering the potential savings on paper and toner if the measure was narrower.

From this quick sketch, I worked up a larger, full-size sketch to get an idea of proportion of type areas, rules and white space.

Working at this full size, in pen and paper, gives an immediate idea of the scale of the elements on the page. I really would recommend this for when you design print alternatives for your websites. Draw it out on paper first. It's quick and will save you a lot of time in the long run.

Quickly sketching the thumbnails allows me to solve design problems with minimum investment.

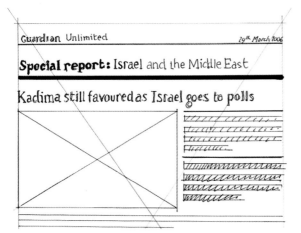

Digitising and colour

I then took the sketch and worked it up in Photoshop, (you could use InDesign or Illustrator if you like), to use the typeface I wanted and to add colour.

Guardian Unlimited   *29th March 2006*

Special report: Israel and the Middle East

Kadima still favoured as Israel goes to polls

Labour party leader Amir Peretz and his wife Achlama cast their votes in Israeli general elections. Photograph: David Furst/EPA

Israelis are today voting in a general election many expect will result in a government with a mandate to set the final borders of the Jewish state.

Opinion polls suggest Kadima, the party set up by the stricken Israeli prime minister,

Ariel Sharon, will see off the opposition unless there is unexpected surge to the right.

As Israelis voted, an explosion near a farming community in southern Israel killed an adult and a child who were reportedly Arab shepherds in a field.

Rescue officials said either a Palestinian rocket attack or stray ordnance near the border with the Gaza Strip had caused the blast.

The Islamic Jihad militant group claimed responsibility, saying the explosion had been timed to disrupt the election, the Associated Press reported. In the past, Palestinian violence has driven Israeli voters towards hardline parties.

The acting Israeli prime minister, Ehud Olmert of Kadima, cast his vote as the polls opened amid high security at 7am local time (0600 BST).

Go out and vote, all of Israel, a smiling Mr Olmert said, referring to predictions that many Israelis would shun the election because they see the result as a foregone conclusion.

Seven hours after voting began, 30.9% of Israel's 4.5 million eligible voters had cast their ballots, the Central Elections Committee said. That figure was nearly 4% below levels from the last election, in 2003, and analysts said a low turnout could hit Kadima's prospects.

The first exit polls are expected after voting ends at 10pm local time.

The election is widely seen as a referendum on the future of the West Bank, which Israel has occupied for 39 years.

Mr Olmert plans to withdraw unilaterally from most Israeli settlements in the West Bank if the Palestinians, and their new Hamas government, fail to become "partners for peace".

In a newspaper article published today, he said no Jewish settlements would be left east of Israel's West Bank security wall if, as expected, Kadima became the main element in a new coalition government.

Working at this full size, and then printing it out, gave me a template on which to base my CSS measurements. Remember, with the printed page we are dealing with absolutes again, rather than fluid layouts or differences in browsers. You can define type size, leading and measurements, which all exist in a finite space: a piece of paper.

I found that completing this stage of the process really helped in pulling the styles together later on.

The finished article

This shows the finished printed article page shown next to an open spread of the paper. As you can see, it shows a continuation of the brand and the content is presented clearly and legibly.

A few rules of thumb

This is a bit of a disclaimer. Most browsers print differently –
wildly. If you develop a print stylesheet, with an intricate layout on
Safari, and then print it using IE on a PC, chances are, it will break.

Although it's possible to create fantastic layouts using CSS and
print media stylesheets, the reality is, you have to keep it
fairly simple.

• Avoid using absolute positioning.

• Use points for your type measurements. For printed text,
standard 9–12 pt type is considered optimal for legibility.

• For line–height of 9–12 pt type, set the value to the type–size
plus 1 to 4 pt. Incidentally, in graphic design, 9 pt type
with 13 pt leading is written in shorthand as 9/13, (which
looks like CSS, but isn't), and is spoken as 'nine on thirteen'.

• Consider changing your markup. Your html markup is not
sacred. If there is a need for print stylesheets, then adding
class names–such as 'standfirst' to a `<p>` tag – is
perfectly acceptable.

• Optimise to black, white and grey. By all means make your
printed page in colour, but be careful of legibility when it is
just printed in black and white. Always check it first because
many readers will be using black and white printers.

• Experiment with typefaces. Some typefaces don't work on
screen, but work very well in print and are available on
almost every computer, (Zapf Chancery, for example).

• Don't use too much black. You'll waste loads of toner and your
users will hate you.

• Always set type smaller than you think. The default type size
in Microsoft Word is 12pt. That's the largest you really should
have to set text.

A final word

Typography has suffered from the advent of technology, (and I'm not just talking about computers here). Designers on the whole have divorced themselves from the letterforms and the setting of them. As a result, they've forgotten, or not been made aware of, the simple typesetting rules which were core to the old system of printers' apprenticeship.

Typography to me is about design. It's about words and the conveyance of meaning. It's about setting words that people read. A certain amount of it is creative, a certain amount is expression and aesthetics, but mostly, it's about people reading stuff. Do them a favour and don't make it difficult.

Colour

Design and Colour is a monsterous topic. I'm certainly not going to cover it all in this section, but that's not the intention. This book is about the basics of graphic design as it applies to the web and, as such, I'm going to take what I feel is useful in colour theory and just present and explain that. Colour theory can be complicated because, over time, it has come to represent three areas of study: scientific, artistic and psychological.

Within this chapter, I'm just going to talk about one area – artistic – and touch on another, psychological. I'm not going to be discussing the science of colour and how that applies to things like accessibility on the web; whole books have been written on that subject alone.

Designing with colour is perhaps the element of graphic design which is the most difficult to get right. Why? Because it is the most subjective. For some, a palette of dark grey with splashes of bright pink will be just great; to others it would just be all wrong. Too many designers, whether schooled in colour theory or not, end up making subjective decisions about colour and then when it comes to explaining those decisions to a client, things begin to unravel.

This chapter will help you move beyond the subjective and provide you with the foundation you need to make objective decisions. It's about getting to grips with simple colour theory, creating effective colour combinations and making sure you don't offend a traditional Chinese wedding company by designing their website in predominantly white *(which is associated with funerals, by the way).*

4

Chapter Sixteen
The Colour Wheel

Colour theory involves a great deal of complex terminology; in this chapter, I'll outline some of the basics.

At its heart, colour theory is concerned with the creation of colour combinations via relationships. The relationships are created by the position of the colours on the colour wheel.

The complexity of colour theory really kicks in when you start taking into account different hues, shades and tones. It can all get a bit too much. So here, I'm keeping things very simple and I'm starting at the beginning with primary colours.

Primary Colours

Primary colours can be divided into two different types: additive and subtractive. The additive primaries are those which are obtained by light: red, green and blue. They combine to form white and form the basis of colours on screen, (your TV works in RGB, as does your computer screen). Subtractive primaries are those obtained by the subtraction of light: cyan, magenta and yellow. They form the basis of 'four colour' printing and combine to form black, the K in CMYK.

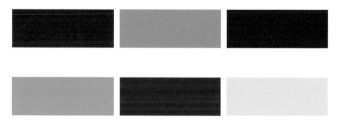

Primary colours:
Red, Green, Blue, and Cyan, Magenta, and Yellow.

left: **Subtractive colours** combine to form black.

right: **Additive colours** reduce to produce white.

The Colour Wheel

The colour wheel not only helps understand the relationship of different colours but also the classification of colours. It also, as I said, provides a quick reference to the primary, secondary and tertiary hues.

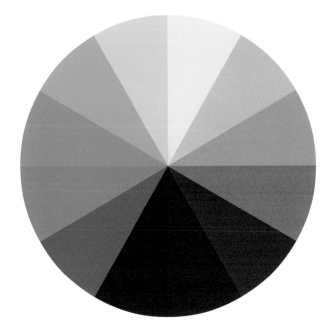

The Colour Wheel

Primary, secondary and tertiary colours

The primary, secondary and tertiary hues are shown in the diagram below. As you can see, it's pretty straight-forward to see how each is produced; primary colours combined create secondary colours. Tertiary colours are created by combining a Primary and a Secondary. Things start to get interesting when you isolate different combinations of colours and this is when we get into the realms of colour wheel selections.

left: **Primary**
right: **Secondary**
bottom: **Tertiary**

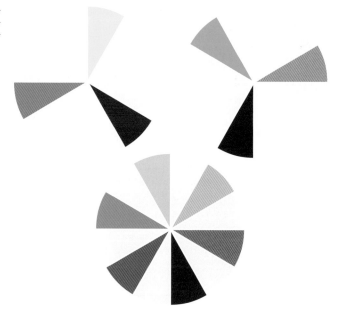

Colour Wheel selections

Colours, when selected from the colour wheel in certain combinations, interact together. This is the basis of colour palettes; the interaction of colours. Knowing the basis of these colour combination types is essential in creating palettes.
True, you can rely on gut instinct, (as many designers do), but more often than not these decisions are based on experience of seeing these colour combinations everywhere in everyday life. Really, once you start to notice these different combinations, it will drive you bonkers.

Monochrome

Monochrome selections are simply one colour from the colour wheel.

Monochrome can be any colour from the colour wheel

Complementary

Complementary selections are based on contrasting colours.
Sometimes they look horrible and simply do not work.
However, sometimes they are just the ticket. I generally use them
if I want a vibrancy in a palette, or if I need to draw the readers
eye to something. Hues of these colours work great as a highlight
colour. They are defined by the colours opposing each other on
the colour wheel.

Complementary colours
are defined by the colours
opposing each other on the
colour wheel.

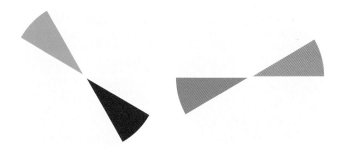

Triads

Triads are really interesting. They provide tension, which can be
important in some designs, because their strength is relatively
equal. Triad colours are any three colours which are equidistant
on the colour wheel. As all three colours contrast with one another
they can clash and this is where the tension is created.

Triad colours are any
three colours which are
equidistant on the
colour wheel.

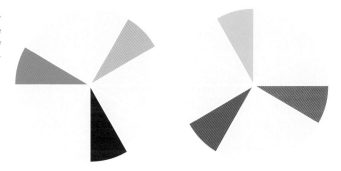

Other Colour Wheel selections

There are other selections which can be used to form palettes:
Analogous, Mutual complements, near complements and
double complements.

> 'Colours, when selected from from the colourwheel in
> certain combinations, interact together. This is the basis of
> colour palettes; the interaction of colours.'

Analogous colours, for example, are those which sit immediately
adjacent on either side of a selected colour on the wheel. However,
I find that I rarely use these four types of colour wheel selections
consciously. Designers are more likely to choose these selections
unconsciously, as they appear around us naturally.

Chapter Seventeen
Hue, Saturation and Brightness

Describing colour can often be confusing. How would you describe brown? Darker than red, or more muddy than peach but with a bit of red in it, oh and some yellow.

Having some standard terms to help you describe and organise colour would be a useful thing at this point. Enter hue, saturation and brightness.

Hue, saturation and brightness are ways to organise and describe colours.

Hue

Hue refers to a specific tone of colour. It is not another name for colour as colour can have saturation and brightness as well as a hue.

A **Hue** can be any tone or shade of any colour on the **Colour Wheel.**

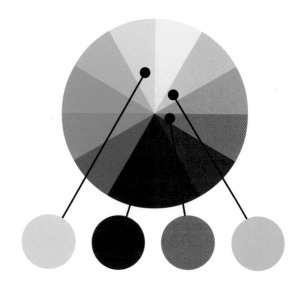

Saturation

Saturation refers to the purity, or intensity of a colour. It is the intensity of a hue from grey. At maximum saturation a colour would contain no grey at all. At minimum saturation, a colour would contain mostly grey.

More Grey *No Grey*

Brightness

Brightness refers to how much white, or black, is contained within a colour.

More White *Less White*

More Black *Less Black*

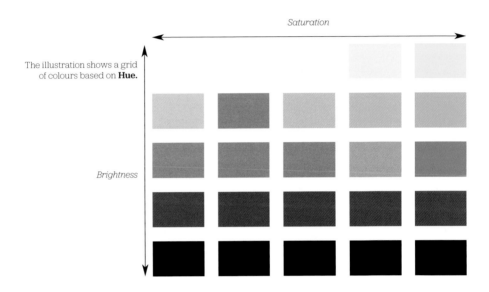

Saturation

The illustration shows a grid of colours based on **Hue.**

Brightness

The illustration above shows the difference between saturation and brightness. We first pick a hue from the colour wheel and then reduce the saturation so that the colour becomes more and more grey. Then picking a lesser saturated tone, you can see that by adding white or black, the brightness of the hue is affected.

An important thing to notice is that increasing brightness is not the same as decreasing saturation. Decreasing saturation turns the colours into shades of grey, increasing brightness turns the hue lighter but without making it grey.

This can be seen more clearly when the same theory is applied to a photograph.

Here you can see a photograph which has had no tampering on the left. First of all, I'm going to decrease the saturation of the yellows in the photograph. You can see that the yellows have now turned to greys.

left: Original

right: **Decreased Saturation** of Yellow.

If I increased the brightness at this point, the yellows retain their new grey feeling, but just become lighter. Similarly if I decrease the brightness – in effect add black – then the yellows retain their grey colouring and just turn darker.

left: **Decreased Saturation**
of Yellow.

right: **Increased Brightness**
of de-Saturated yellow

Now, If I take the original photograph again and increase the saturation of the yellow, the yellows become more pure and more vibrant but more importantly, they become more pure and more vibrant because they contain less grey. I'll go through the same process again and alter the brightness. The colours, as you would expect, retain their new saturation but the white and black content is altered accordingly.

left: Original

right: **Increased Saturation**
of yellow

left: **Increased Saturation**
of yellow

right: **Increased Brightness**
of **Saturated** yellow

Chapter Eighteen
Colour combinations and mood

Colours chosen from different spokes on the Colour Wheel will provide a variety of colour combinations. Deciding upon and selecting a colour combination that works will very much depend upon the job at hand.

Will it communicate what you want it to? Or, are you just choosing it because you, or the client, like it? These are difficult questions to answer because any designer or client will let their personal style and preference interfere with their decision-making. Colour combinations tend to evoke certain reactions, based on cultural or personal experience. Understanding these experiences will help you create colour combinations that tell a story. That is what good colour theory can give you: designs that tell a story.

I'm going to go over a few combinations here to demonstrate my thinking, but before I get onto that, it's worth noting how palettes can be presented to potential clients or in design documentation.

Presenting Combinations and Palettes

I've always presented palettes in two different ways depending on the amount of colours. In a broad palette, with many colours, I display these left to right with dominance and usage being denoted by the size of the square, or block, of colour. For smaller palettes and combinations, I use the rectangle containing a line and a square. I was taught this simple device in university but it is similar to many other examples I've seen. You can use circles, blobs, lines, squares. It's up to you. The important thing is to indicate the relative weight of colour.

I was tempted to call this combination a Triad. However, if you think back to the Colour Wheel, this is not the case.

In colour theory, "triads" aren't just any combination of three colours. Triads are based on colours which are equidistant on the Colour Wheel.

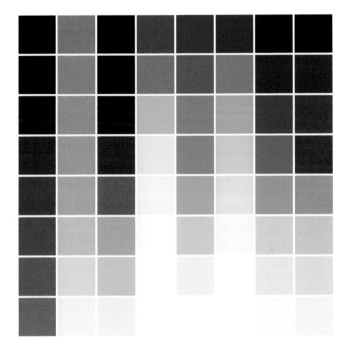

Colour palette showing range of colours and relative weight.

1. **Subordinate, or base colour.** *This is a visually weak or subordinate colour. It should contrast or complement.*

2. **Dominant or main colour.** *This colour defines the communicative values of the combination.*

3. **Accent or highlight colour.** *The accent colour can be sympathetic to the subordinate or dominant colour. Or, instead, you may choose an accent colour that is visually strong and striking, and appears to compete with the dominant colour. This can provide tension within a combination.*

Examples of Colour Combinations

Active / Vibrant

Active combinations are intense. They feature bright, often complementary, colours on the colour wheel and are combinations of primary, secondary and tertiary colours. To many people, colour combinations such as this evoke feelings of noise, flamboyance and energy. It's a young combination, (although not in all cultures), aimed at young adults. Usually these colors aren't the ones I describe as 'natural' on the next page, although they may be more intense tones of those same colours – and therefore, useful for 'natural' applications, such as the travel industry.

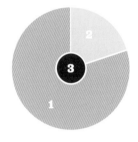

Colour combination showing
Subordinate, Dominant and
Accent colours

1. Subordinate or base colour
2. Dominant or main colour
3. Accent or highlight colour

Muted / Calm

Muted palettes have a lot of white in the hues. This example uses blues and introduces lavender as the dominant colour. The resultant colourway, (or combination), is balanced and calming. Hues in the blue, green and violet areas of the colour wheel convey a visual quietness. The accent is almost always used as sympathetic to the dominant. Often used in the cosmetics industry, the visual softness of the colours usually portrays a feminine quality.

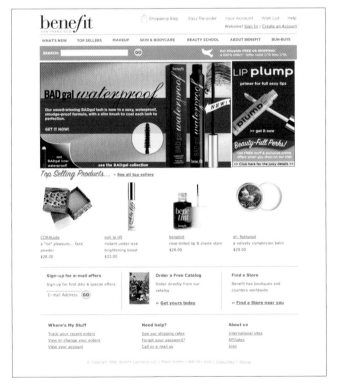

Benefit Cosmetics use of Calm colours

Pastel

A pastel combination is similar to the muted combination, in that it is often based on colours containing a lot of white, (or lack of white, if you are using the subtractive CMYK colour model used in print work). Where they differ is that pastel combinations combine warm and cool tones readily. This combination can portray youth and innocence, (babies!), and has a warmth that the muted combination fails to deliver.

Coolspotters use of Pastel colours throughout

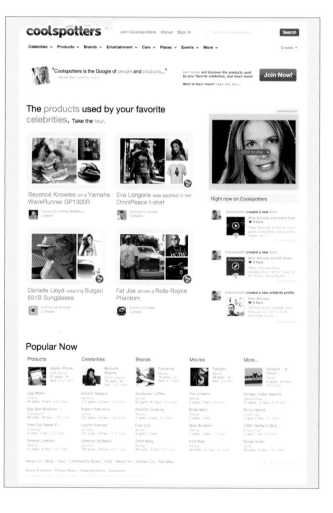

Natural

Natural combinations are those colours that are borrowed from the great outdoors. Rusty reds, browns, sky blues and warm pinks are the order of the day. I find the easiest way to create these combinations is to go outside, take a photograph and then choose some colours from that; you really can create some stunning combinations. When you need to communicate rustic charm or the feeling of walking through autumn leaves, then this is the type of combination you're after.

The Body Shop's use of natural colours

Rich

This is a good one: hues of royalty, tradition, (often religious), and, above all, wealth. Rich colour combinations are the combinations which are so engrained in culture. True, the actual colours used may differ, but the overall effect is seen throughout the world. Maroon is often mixed with gold and strong shades of green. For a fuller palette, add colours from the natural combination described earlier.

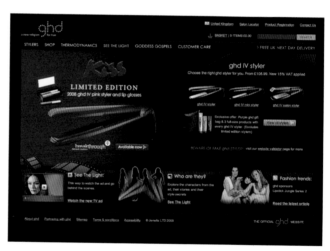

ghd's use of rich colours

Part of the Design Solution

I hope I've conveyed what an important role colour plays in the design solution. By selecting the best combination of colours, you can go a long way toward ensuring the success of your design.

We've looked at some colour combinations here, but what about the individual colours? They communicate their own meanings and make a significant impact on the mood and tone of a given design. Next, I'll move on to discussing colour and mood. What do individual colours mean?

Moody Stories

Colours can tell a story in a very effective way because they create an emotional reaction from the reader. These reactions can form the basis of how a design is perceived. So, if a design uses a lot of red and orange, it could be described as 'angry', 'hot', 'wealth', 'divine' or 'pure'. The latter two in this list account for cultural differences in interpretation of the colour red. In the same way, a design which is comprised of a predominantly blue colour combination could be described as 'cold', 'calm' or 'reserved'.

Designers must be sensitive to the cultural aspects of the meaning and symbolism of colours. Let's take the example I've just used of red. In the West, red is seen as a hot colour. It's vibrant, flashy, and angry. In fact, a common saying is 'seeing red', or 'the red mist descends', indicating anger or fury. However, in the East, red is seen as a colour associated with wealth, purity and good fortune and sometimes divinity. Another great example is black and white. In the West, black can be associated with death and mourning. The opposite is sometimes the case in the East; white is the colour of mourning.

Choosing colours should therefore not only be an exercise in finding the right balance and aesthetic combination of colours, but also an exercise in studying the target audience's cultural norms. The consequences of getting it wrong could be disastrous.

Colours that aren't colours

Black

In looking at the connection between colour and mood, we begin with a colour that isn't really a colour. Black is the absence of colour. In the West, it's associated with death and mourning, but also has an authoratitive, official feel. It can sometimes be used in branding to give a sense of style; a classy touch. In this sense, black can suggest wealth and oppulance. Black should be used sparingly, though, especially on the web, due to its value of perceived weight. A user will always think a black web page loads quicker than a white one.

White

White, too, isn't a colour. Again, there are cultural differences. In the East, white is associated with funerals, death and mourning. In the West, the opposite is the case, where white is associated with simplicity, purity and goodness. We see white everywhere in branding, businesses and buildings where we want to feel calm. White is perhaps the most important component of most colour palettes because it provides a base colour on which all other colours will work.

Primaries

Red

As discussed, red is an interesting subject. In the West: hot,
passionate and demanding attention and in the East: good fortune,
wealth and purity. It is also a tricky colour to use effectively in a
design because of its strength and vibrancy. It is often used as
an accent colour, to draw the attention of a user or reader. When
darkened to wine red or burgundy, it has a classier feel, especially
when coupled with warm oranges and golden yellows. Lighten
it up and you get pink. I've always struggled with pink as a
colour. I find it incredibly difficult to use unless it is part of a
pastel combination.

Blue

Blue is a strong colour. Associated with a calm and soothing
feeling, when darkened to navy it can also convey traditional
values. Blue works well with white, and has a wide range of tones
which also work well with a large variety of colour combinations.
It can be used to elicit a feeling of trust when combined with
grey. Modern palettes can be created by adding lime green or
a calming lilac. Paler blues, more in the pastel range of tones,
suggest a youthfulness so often seen in products for baby boys; it
seems that everything designed for them is powder blue.

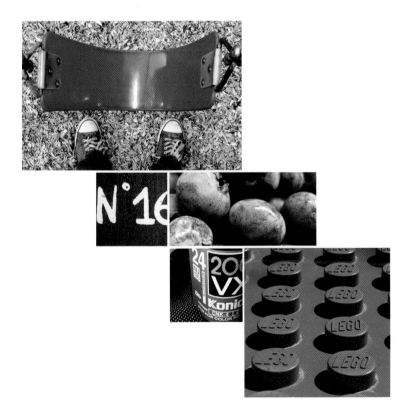

Yellow

Yellow is a cheerful and bright colour. In its purest form, it has associations with nature, childhood, the sun and happiness. However, add red to it and you start to move towards autumnal feelings. Add green to it and things go a bit horrible; associations with disease and illness. The best advice for yellow is to take it easy; don't use too much. When coupled with black, yellow is the highest contrast colour, which is why you see it on so many warning signs, airport signage, and so many other signage systems. We are, of course, just copying nature here, bees and wasps use these colours to great effect.

Green

A natural colour, green suggests fields, grass, and trees and with this, a sense of calm and well-being. It's commonly used on environmentally-friendly products for the same reason. It can also be very vibrant when combined with black and other primary colours such as red.

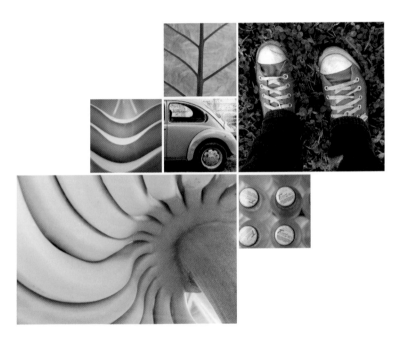

Secondaries and Tertiaries

Orange

As orange has its basis in red and yellow, it shares some of the
characteristics of its parents. It's a hot colour, but playful in a way
red isn't. This is the youthful yellow in the colour. Orange also
features highly in natural colour combinations along with greens
and browns. The associated feeling of changing seasons, growth
and warmth inspire its use alongside green in packaging for
organic produce, for example.

Brown

Also a natural colour, brown can be used as a replacement for black in a natural colour combination. In fact, the impressionist artists of the late 19th century did just that. The warmth and vibrancy in paintings by Monet is largely due to black being replaced by browns and purples. So, if you want to warm up your palette, get rid of black and replace it with dark brown – especially if you have other natural colours present.

Purple

Purple is a royal colour. Used with golden yellows and light lime greens, it can suggest royalty and wealth. Combine it with red and orange, and purple tempers the heat of the two other colours, in this case it can provide depth. Purple is also associated with the feeling of mystery and imagination. Because of this, it is regularly used in children's products.

A lot of this may seem a bit 'away with the fairies' and at too high a level for the average design project. But the meaning, and cultural differences, of different colours really can help inform a design's colour combination.

Chapter Nineteen
Designing without colour

Lowering the Tone

Years ago, when I was in my first year on a Foundation Art and Design course in Stockport in the UK, I wanted to be a painter, (well, an illustrator, to be precise). In the first week of this course we were all told to get rid of our nice new paintbrushes that we'd just purchased for the course. We were told to leave all our new kit at home and to go outside and find some nice twigs and get some black ink from somewhere. I was not chuffed. How was an artist meant to create with these primitive tools?

The lecturers had us painting with twigs, our feet, blindfolded – the works. At the time I hated it; I couldn't see the point. Now, I look back and really see the value of this horrific couple of weeks. They were teaching us how to look and produce marks that weren't dictated to by our tools. In other words, because we had colourful paints and lovely sable brushes, the temptation is to use them. Without the brushes and the colourful paint, we were forced into trying to communicate colour with tone alone.

Removing Colour

One of the things I like about editorial design, specifically typographic design, is the emphasis on black and white. True, colour is a very important part of any typographic exercise, but primarily I begin by looking at tone and form. I think there's a lot of value in removing colour from the equation entirely and focussing on the tonal aspects of a design before applying the colour.

There are a few notable examples of how designing with just black make for a unique and attractive design.

Of course, no discussion about designing with black and white on the web would be complete without mentioning Khoi Vinh's site, Subtraction.com. Khoi works with black and white and

accents of orange, (in his navigational rollovers), to harmonise
with the spare, grid-based Swiss undertones of the design.

Khoi Vinh's
Subtraction.com is a prime
example of how to use black
and white effectively

Form, a German design magazine, uses black and white typography, (and a strong grid), to convey its brand to the users of the site. By choosing black and white for the framework of the magazine, any showcased, full-colour work really stands out.

German design magazine, **Form.** Full colour works very well against a backdrop of stark black and white

Begin with grey

Next time you start a design, try to follow my simple heading: Begin your design using only tones of grey. Don't introduce any colour until the design is working in black and white. Chances are, your decisions on palette and colour will be made a lot easier because the design – or elements of the design – aren't relying on colour for their function or meaning. This of course is very useful for designing with accessibility in mind. I'm not addressing any accessibility issues within these articles, as I'd like to focus on the graphic design, but it's an important consideration that shouldn't be overlooked. Designing with black and white first will ensure that the solution doesn't rely on colour to work.

I often use colour to highlight specific elements of the design, but generally those elements have a function within the design solution, such as the horizontal lines on this site. Another example might be highlighting a search button, or elements of a navigation bar. Using colour to pick out key functional elements in the interface.

The benefit of working this way, like other tools at the disposal of designers such as grid systems, is that it solves a certain amount of problems for the designer. I find it focusses my attention on tone and composition so that I needn't worry if this colour matches that. Focus on the composition's tone and, once that's sorted, move on to the colour.

Chapter Twenty
Colour and Brand

Can you imagine a classic coke can in any other colour? How about the golden arches of McDonald's - can you see them in blue?

The essense of the brand is expressed through that single colour. Consumers rely on that colour recognition to make a choice about a brand. One of my favourite branding stories is about colour.

Michael Wolff, of the famous branding consultancy Wolff Olins, was invited to pitch for the original rebranding of British Petroleum (BP). There was tough competition from some of the brightest branding companies on the planet. But Michael Wolff had the nerve to give a presentation with no words, no brand strategy document, no hint of new logo. He just showed slides of rolling fields and trees. He proposed BP owned the colour green. The colour green would be the linchpin for the rebranding exercise.

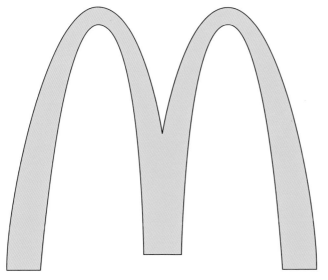

top: **Coca Cola**'s famous red hand script

bottom: **McDonalds** famous golden arches

BP took this a step further when they merged with Amoco in 1998. They 'needed to reinvent the energy business, to go beyond petroleum, not by abandoning oil and gas, but by improving the ways in which it is used and produced so our business is aligned with the long-term needs of the world.' (Lord John Browne, Group Chief Executive, BP).

Landor Associates were tasked with the redesign. BP has such a strong brand, the green was retained and built upon with a new positioning, 'Beyond Petroleum', and a new logo which took the relationship with nature a step further.

left: Old **BP** Logo
Right: New **BP** Logo

Colour expresses personality

Colour is used in branding to evoke a reaction and stimulate brand association.

The Orange brand was created in 1994 for Hutchison Telecom's UK mobile phone network. Immediately, the brand was distinctive, fresh and appealing to the target market. The brand used primarily Helvetica as the typeface, but it was the simple, bold and consistent colour usage that made the bold statement in a brand marketplace. The orange colour was often coupled with white, or black, presenting a simple, sophisticated image. The resultant modernist appearance appealed to a certain audience demographic; mostly young, professional men with a high disposable income. Orange were perhaps the first mobile phone network to introduce style in order to sell phones. They were an aspirational brand; they wanted people to aspire to use their products. They built this up through advertising, marketing, sponsorship and careful product placement. Throughout all of this activity, the primary vehicle in brand recognition was a colour: orange.

Colour brand basics

Own a colour

As discussed earlier in this chapter, owning a colour is the holy grail of brand identity.

Use colour to build meaning

In chapter thirteen, I described the various meanings colours have. If you can align your brand, or design, with a colour that makes sense, this will reinforce the meaning of your design.

Develop the best tools to get consistency of colour

On the web, we have good standards for colour reproduction – RGB and Hex values. The only down side is the discrepancies between monitors. LCD screens tend to wash colour out – specifically pastel tones. PC's and Apple Macs have different gamma settings – PCs generally being slightly darker and richer in tone. Ensuring colour is consistent across all of these devices is impossible, but you should still stick to the standards. Any slight deviation can undermine a brand.

Consistency across all media

Not only do different monitors display slightly different colours, as described over leaf, but different media display colours differently. For example, mobile phones may have different screen settings. TV and cinema screens, different compression codecs in video compression can affect colour. Make sure you know the problems, and design for the middle ground.

Be careful with colour coding

You may decide to assign different sub-brand colours to different sections of a website. Colour coding different sub-brands is a common practice, but depending on the amount of sub-brands, can quickly turn into a nightmare. You see, there aren't enough colours with suitable contrast – you can quickly run out. To circumvent this, build a brand that does not rely solely on colours to determine differentiation.

Colour usage should be a considered design decision as part of the broader design process. Your colour choices can be based on your intuition, or by following some of the theory I've discussed – both are correct approaches. Your intuition will be informed by colour you see around you and you may be surprised at how it closely it follows the theory.

When working with clients, or other members of a team, be mindful that every one has a favourite colour, or one they hate. It's your job – however difficult – to provide considered rationale for choosing a particular colour. It shouldn't be because you like it, but because it's the *right* choice.

Layout

Laying out a website design is where all of the different aspects of web design come into play. From research, information architecture, and user experience design through to the typography, colour and grid systems. Creating a layout combines all of these, but as web designers, we have to factor in other variables such as browser type, screen size and resolution. Do you go fixed width, liquid, or elastic? What about other media types like print? What about other devices such as the iPhone?

Creating layouts for the web can be a headache. With such a bewildering array of choices before us, I've found time and time again that going back to basics – at least initially – helps enormously in designing layouts. By using simple tools of composition, combined with good typography and colour usage, you can achieve a lot with your designs.

It's very easy to become distracted by modern web design. The speed at which this medium evolves is sometimes terrifying, and with it, the perceived job of a web designer evolves too. I know sometimes I've felt overwhelmed, confused, and directionless: 'Should I learn Javascript?', 'What about CSS3?', 'How do I find time to do all of this?' Sound familiar? At times like this – and I do find myself asking those questions from time to time – I go back to basics. I go back to composition theory, and colour basics. I refresh myself with the nuances of setting headlines. I get back to what I fell in love with in the first place, and layout is one of those things.

5

Chapter Twenty–One
The Basics of Composition

For centuries there has been a link between art and mathematics, but how can you quantify beauty? How can you create a formula for aesthetic appeal? Philosophers, mathematicians, architects and artists have tried to answer these questions for thousands of years.

During art college I was subjected to a lecture on the Golden Section, (who remembers that lecture, come on hands up?), that ambiguous set of rectangles that is requisite art school discussion. During this lecture I was shown slide after slide of seemingly tenuous links between paintings and sculptures, and this set of rectangles. My lecturer at the time seemed as equally uninterested, droning along in self-imposed boredom. What he failed to convey at the time, has taken me over 15 years to even begin to understand. So what is the importance of these boring rectangles and how do they relate to design?

The Golden Section

Many theories on aesthetic measurement have their basis in numerical patterns that occur naturally such as the proportions of the human body, for example the distance between your elbow and the tip of your fingers compared to the distance between your elbow and your wrist. Theories, such as the Golden Section, (and its many other names), arise from these natural patterns and they are applied to art, (either consciously or subconsciously), to create 'beauty' by way of considered composition.

The Golden Section, Golden Ratio, and the grandiose Divine Proportion are all names for the same thing; a ratio of 1.618. Nodding off? Not yet? Good! Bear with me. Here's the math: the

Golden Ratio is the ratio between two segments so that the ratio between point ac/bc is 1.618.

This may not seem that important, but the Golden Section is found throughout nature, mathematics, architecture, art and design. It is derived from a naturally occurring number, called Phi, which has intrigued humanity for thousands of years.
Many usages of the Golden Section in art – and architecture specifically – were no doubt by complete accident. Artists and architects are visually–aware people. Those early experimenters were in tune with the proportions of their surroundings and incorporated what they saw into their art. They did it because it felt right. And it's this word, 'felt', that interests me.

Throughout art school I was taught to 'feel' my way round composition. I was taught that when something was right, it 'felt' right. This school of thought went all the way up through college to university and my first job as a designer. Composition was about feel, not thought. This seemed to go against the very nature of what I understood to be design communication and problem solving.

The biggest problem with the Golden Section is the mathematics involved. Using the ratio as a basis for deriving layout measurements is, frankly, a bit of a nightmare. Very quickly, you can end up with unworkable numbers. This is where the Rule of Thirds comes in.

The Rule of Thirds

Photographers have used the Rule of Thirds for years, who borrowed it from, yet again, classical artists and architects. The theory is simple – which is why it's easy to apply in your day-to-day design work. Divide any workspace, or layout, into thirds horizontally and vertically, and align key focus points of your composition to where the lines intersect.

The Rule of Thirds is easier to use than the Golden Section. The simple division of space can easily be applied to designing for the web. For fixed width designs, (E.g., 960px wide), the space can be broken down into three 320px columns. For fluid designs – those that use percentages for layout – they can be divided into 33% columns. The challenge, however, for applying this theory to modern web design, is that we can't be sure on the vertical space. This is where subdividing the Rule of Thirds comes in handy.

On a web page, we can't be sure how long a page will be.
Therefore, we can't apply the Rule of Thirds to the vertical space,
but, we can attempt to put some loose guidelines in place.

We start by dividing the 960px wide 'page' into thirds, giving
us three, equal columns of 320px wide. We also use the same
measurements vertically. This will give us nine equal squares of
320px by 320px. What I'm really interested in here, is seeing how
we can use this simple sub-division to create guidelines for nearer
the top of the page - this is where a designer will have the most
control of vertical space.

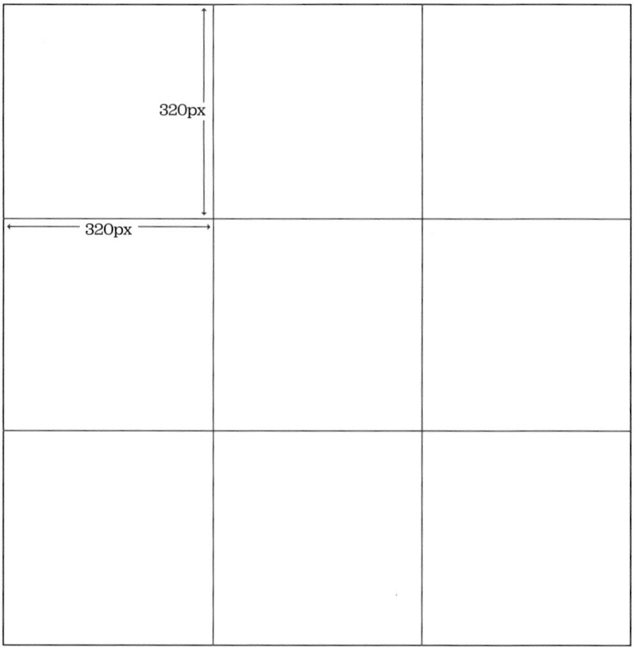

320px

320px

Now, I sub-divide each square into nine equal squares. I'm slightly jumping ahead of myself here, as this is now starting to look like a grid, and I'm going to come onto talking about that in a couple of chapters time.

The only problem with this is that we start getting odd numbers cropping up. 320px divided by 3 is 106.66666. We can simplify this by rounding up to 107, but having the last division as 106. Remember, this is only for approximate guidelines for layout.

Now, we have some horizontal lines that we can use as a basis for laying out elements on the vertical plane. The same process can be done with percentages for fluid width designs. The beauty of this process is that vertical space is now not based on any arbitrary values. There is a direct relationship between anything aligned to these lines, to the overall width of the design, to the width of the columns, to the width of the sub-divisions and so on. Any composition based on this grid will hang off this connected 'skeleton'.

Looking Room

Think back to last night. There you are, settled down in front of the TV, watching your favourite soap opera, with a nice hot cup of tea in hand. Did you notice – whilst engrossed in the latest love-triangle – that the cameraman has worked very hard to support your eye's natural movement on-screen? He's carefully framed individual shots to create balance.

Think back to last week. There you were, sat with your mates watching the big match. Did you notice that the cameraman frames the shot to go with the direction of play? A player moving right will always be framed so that he is on the far left, with plenty of 'room' to run into.

Both of these cameramen use a technique called Looking Room, sometimes called Lead Room. Looking Room is the space between the subject, (be it a football, or a face), and the edge of the screen. Specifically, Looking Room is the negative space on the side the subject is looking or moving towards.

The great thing is, it's not just limited to photography, film or television; we can use it in web design too.

Basic Framing

Before we get into Looking Room, and how it applies to web, we need to have a look at some basics of photographic composition.

Many web sites use imagery, or photographs, to enhance the content. But even with professionally-shot photographs, without a basic understanding of framing or composition, you can damage how the image is perceived.

A simple, easy way to make photographs more interesting is to fill the frame.

Take this rather mundane photograph of a horse:

By closely cropping, and filling the frame, we can instantly change the mood of the shot.

I've also added Looking Room on the right of the horse. This is space that the horse would be walking into. It gives the photograph 'movement'.

Subject, Space, and Movement

Generally speaking, a portrait photograph will have a subject and space around them. Visual interest in portrait photography can come from movement; how the eye moves around the shot. To get the eye moving, the photographer modifies the space around the subject.

Look at this portrait:

The photographer has framed the subject on the right, allowing for whitespace, or Looking Room, in the direction the subject is looking. The framing of the subject (1), with the space to the left (2) – the Looking Room – creates movement, shown by the arrow (3).

Note the subject is not framed centrally, (shown by the lighter dotted line).

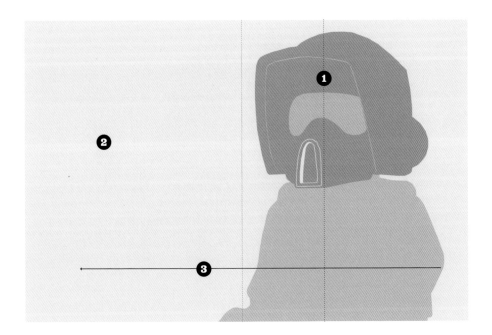

If the photographer had framed the subject with equal space either side, (1 & 2), the resulting composition is static, like our horse.

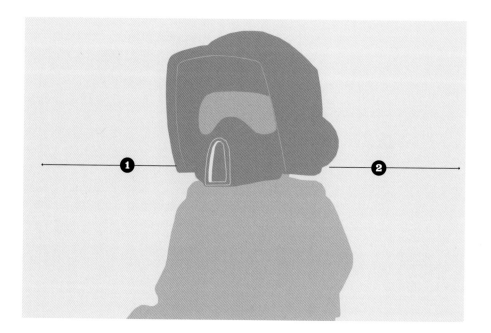

If the photographer framed the subject way over on the left, as the subject is looking that way (1), the resulting whitespace on the right (2) leads to a very uncomfortable composition.

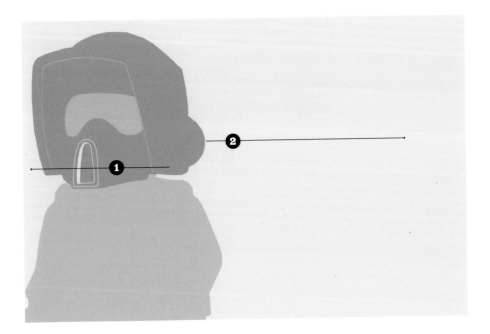

The root of this discomfort is what the framing is telling our eye to do. The subject, looking to the left, suggests to us that we should do the same. However, the Looking Room on the right is telling our eye to occupy this space. The result is a confusing back and forth.

How Looking Room applies to the web

We can apply the same theory to laying out a web page or application. Taking the three same elements – Subject, Space, and resulting Movement – we can guide a user's eye to the elements we need to. As designers, or content editors, framing photographs correctly can have a subtle but important effect on how a page is visually scanned.

Take this example:

The BBC homepage uses great photography as a way of promoting content. Here, they have cropped the main photograph to guide the user's eye into the content.

By applying the same theory, the designer or content editor has applied considerable Looking Room (2) to the photograph to create balance with the overall page design, but also to create movement of the user's eye toward the content (1)

If the image was flipped horizontally, the Looking Room is now on the right. The subject of the photograph is looking off the page, drawing the user's eye away from the content. Once again, this results in a confusing back and forth as your eye fights its way over to the left of the page.

A little bit of Art Direction

Art Direction can be described as the act or process of managing the visual presentation of content. Art Direction is difficult to do on the web, because content and presentation are, more often than not, separated. But where there are images, and when we know the templates that those images will populate, we can go a little way to bridging the gap between content and presentation.

By understanding the value of framing and Looking Room, and the fact that it extends beyond just a good looking photograph, we can start to see photography playing more of an integral role in the communication of content. We won't just be populating templates. We'll be art directing.

The Triangle

The humble triangle is a powerful aid in composing layouts. For centuries, the triangle has been used to guide the eye of the reader or viewer, particularly in fine art. The Last Supper, by Leonardo da Vinci, is perhaps one of the most well known paintings to use triangles as a primary compositional device.

In order to guide the onlooker's eye to the main subject of the painting – Jesus Christ – Da Vinci created whitespace, in the form of a triangle either side of Him. Christ Himself is composed in a triangular pose, with His disciples also adopting triangular poses. A simple, but powerful device for guiding the eye.

This theory has been taken and used in photography, architecture, and graphic design for many years. Having three points of focus on a design provides a balance and subsequent movement of the reader's eye. But how can this theory of composition work on the web? An example of how to use this is on the teaser site for this very book.

The design for the teaser site was purposefully simple. A few colours, a few blocks of flat colour. With so many spare content elements, the challenge is providing enough emphasis to guide the user. I designed it using the triangle, with the three points corresponding to three important content elements; the Five Simple Steps logo in the top left (1), the orange circle letting our readers know when the book would be launched (2), and the yellow book cover (3). The natural movement of the eye is from left to right in the western world, so the user would naturally begin at the Five Simple Steps logo, move over to the orange circle, and then be drawn to the yellow cover.

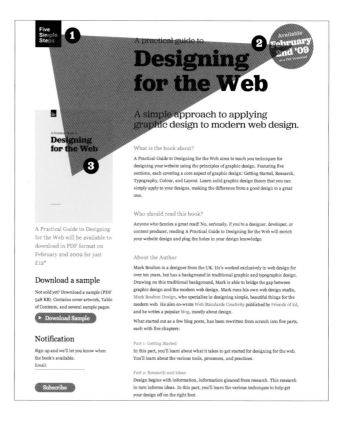

The challenge, when using a triangle as a compositional aid, is ensuring it's not overt and overbearing. The triangle should aid composition, not be evident in the design itself – unless of course, that is the intention. The triangle is such a powerful visual device; there is a danger the readers eye will skip from one point to another without reading, or viewing, the content in–between.

Any compositional tool – such as those I've outlined in this chapter – are there to help. They can provide answers to tricky layout problems. They can go towards making your designs look better. But, unfortunately for us, they're not a quick fix for every project. Just because you use the Golden Section, or compose your layout based on the Rule of Thirds, it doesn't automatically mean it will be effective. These few tools are just meant to be a starting point.

Chapter Twenty–Two
Spatial Relationships

Space is important in layout. Space can be created by content – such as text, images, lists, logos etc. – or it can be created by the space in–between content, called negative space, or whitespace. Space can be passive; a by–product of the layout process. Or, it can be active; there for a reason, to guide the user's eye, or help them make a decision.

Size and Shape

Shapes are elements that can communicate ideas – for example, the BP logo I previously discussed in Part 2. Unusual shapes can attract attention, whilst conventional shapes – when combined with colour – convey meaning. Take a red triangle for example. From computer software, to road traffic signs, a red triangle means warning. Something's wrong. Whereas a green circle, means everything's good. Proceed.

In classical design, there are three types of shape: geometric, natural, and abstract. Geometric shapes are what you'd expect: circles, squares, triangles, rectangles and diamonds. Natural shapes are derived from what we see around us. Abstract shapes can be both representative – impressionistic – or they can be expressionistic. Like the art movements, impressionistic abstract shapes are meant to represent something else. Expressionistic shapes convey meaning, or emotion.

Geometric *Natural* *Abstract*

Shape and size are two of the basic elements of graphic design that determine space. If I change the shape of something, then I'm changing the space around it. If I increase the size of the shape, I decrease the space around it.

Now, all of this is quite abstract at the moment. How can you apply this theory to your every day work? How will knowing the difference between abstract and geometric shapes make any difference to you? Well, it's about learning how to look.

Throughout art school, then through design school, my lecturers and professors would encourage me to view things differently. To simplify my environment into shapes. To look at the space in-between things. To have an appreciation of shape, size, and tone. By looking at the world this way, you can start to understand the richness and complexity of design all around us.

Typographic Colour

Typographic colour refers to the density of type on a page – either a physical page, or on screen. The 'shade' of typographic colour can have an impact on legibility – too dark, with no typographic hierarchy, and your content will be difficult to read. Too light a shade of typographic colour, and your content will also be difficult to read with readers finding it hard to read line to line. But there's plenty you can do to make things easier for your readers.

Let's look at some examples of *dark typographic* colour:

Lorem ipsum dolor sit amet, consectetur adipiscing elit. In a sapien. Cras nec lectus. Donec tristique tristique purus. Ut risus sapien, consectetur sit amet, rhoncus vel, vulputate vel, tortor. Aenean faucibus. Proin vitae sapien. Suspendisse venenatis tempor arcu. Aliquam erat volutpat. Mauris mauris. Proin elit orci, ullamcorper at, placerat vitae, gravida tristique, nibh.

Lorem ipsum dolor sit amet, consectetur adipiscing elit. In a sapien. Cras nec lectus. Donec tristique tristique purus. Ut risus sapien, consectetur sit amet, rhoncus vel, vulputate vel, tortor. Aenean faucibus. Proin vitae sapien. Suspendisse venenatis tempor arcu. Aliquam erat volutpat. Mauris mauris. Proin elit orci, ullamcorper at, placerat vitae, gravida tristique, nibh.

Top: Paragraph set in Helvetica with leading too tight

Bottom: Paragraph set in Garamond Italic with poor letter spacing

The first paragraph here is set in Helvetica. Clearly, the leading – or line-height – is set too small. The second paragraph uses correct leading but italic, serif typefaces generally have letterforms set too closely together.

To correct these two paragraphs, we need to add more leading to the first, and add some letter-spacing to the last. But remember, don't add too much. Type designers have carefully crafted the distances between letterforms. To disrupt that distance is to tamper with the very 'feel' of the typeface, and can have disastrous consequences.

Top: Paragraph set in Helvetica with leading corrected

Bottom: Paragraph set in Garamond Italic with corrected letter spacing

Lorem ipsum dolor sit amet, consectetur adipiscing elit. In a sapien. Cras nec lectus. Donec tristique tristique purus. Ut risus sapien, consectetur sit amet, rhoncus vel, vulputate vel, tortor. Aenean faucibus. Proin vitae sapien. Suspendisse venenatis tempor arcu. Aliquam erat volutpat. Mauris mauris. Proin elit orci, ullamcorper at, placerat vitae, gravida tristique, nibh.

Lorem ipsum dolor sit amet, consectetur adipiscing elit. In a sapien. Cras nec lectus. Donec tristique tristique purus. Ut risus sapien, consectetur sit amet, rhoncus vel, vulputate vel, tortor. Aenean faucibus. Proin vitae sapien. Suspendisse venenatis tempor arcu. Aliquam erat volutpat. Mauris mauris. Proin elit orci, ullamcorper at, placerat vitae, gravida tristique, nibh.

Now, let's look at some examples of *light typographic* colour:

Lorem ipsum dolor sit amet, consectetur adipiscing elit. In a sapien. Cras nec lectus. Donec tristique tristique purus. Ut risus sapien, consectetur sit amet, rhoncus vel, vulputate vel, tortor. Aenean faucibus. Proin vitae sapien. Suspendisse venenatis tempor arcu. Aliquam erat volutpat. Mauris mauris. Proin elit orci, ullamcorper at, placerat vitae, gravida tristique, nibh.

Lorem ipsum dolor sit amet, consectetur adipiscing elit. In a sapien. Cras nec lectus. Donec tristique tristique purus. Ut risus sapien, consectetur sit amet, rhoncus vel, vulputate vel, tortor. Aenean faucibus. Proin vitae sapien. Suspendisse venenatis tempor arcu. Aliquam erat volutpat. Mauris mauris. Proin elit orci, ullamcorper at, placerat vitae, gravida tristique, nibh.

Using the same typefaces as before, this example shows that by setting a paragraph with too much leading, or too much letter-spacing, can also result in an uncomfortable reading experience.

Typefaces themselves can also have a bearing on typographic colour. Some typefaces have wide, open counters, and large spaces between the letterforms, (called kerns). Whilst others have tight counters, with minimal open space in the letterforms. Even the choice of typeface can play a significant role in the typographic colour of your final design.

White Space

My first design job was based in a small studio in Manchester city centre in the UK. It was mostly a print design agency that produced work for various large and small clients alike, in varying media: packaging, publications, marketing support material etc. One of the avenues of output for the studio was Direct Mail.

Designing for Direct Mail is actually quite tricky, for one simple reason: it goes against the fairly sophisticated graphic design principles, which is standard fare in college. Instead, designing Direct Mail is about as sophisticated as a small lump of concrete. Direct-Mail clients want to appear down-market, there is no getting away from the fact that it works as well: big, bold and brash design is the order of the day. And in the words of one client, words that I will never forget as long as I'm a practicing graphic designer; 'White Space is empty space'.

However, for the most part, he couldn't have been further from the truth.

Definition

White, or Negative Space is the space in-between elements in a composition; be that a web page, a web app or a spread in a magazine.

Actually, that's only a part truth. The space between major elements in a composition is Macro White Space. Micro White space, is, yes you've guessed it, the White Space between elements such as list items, the space between a caption and an image, or the space between words and letters.

Macro *white space*   **Micro** *white space*

Legibility

A while ago I was lucky enough to go and see Erik Spiekermann give a lecture. Part of his talk was about his redesign of The Economist magazine. He mentioned one of the primary reasons for the redesign was the Economist thought their design was too heavy. The content was difficult to read.

In newspaper design – which has so many parallels with web design – information is dense. Sometimes, as in web design, it's difficult to add white space because the content makes it hard to do so. Newspapers often deal with this by using a typeface for the body, which is quite light and has plenty of white space within, and around, the characters. This was part of Erik's solution for the redesign of the Economist.

He redesigned the typeface slightly, whilst retaining the quirkiness of the original. He added more whitespace to the individual characters. He set the type slightly smaller I believe, with more leading. All of this was adding Micro White Space to the design. The overall result was subtle. The content was more legible and the overall feeling of the magazine was lighter, yet there was still the same amount of content.

I learnt from Erik that day that, in order to achieve a lightness and an increase in legibility in a design, and this especially applies to the web, you don't have to look at the design at a macro level. Looking at the space between the tiny stuff, at the micro level, can have a big impact on the effectiveness of a design.

White Space helps position brands

For years, designers have been using White Space in their designs
to create a feeling of sophistication for upscale brands. This is
where the Direct Mail client was actually correct in his view on
white space for his product; adding white space to his design would
position his product more upscale than it was.

Coupled with a sensitive use of typography and photography, a
careful use of White Space is seen all over certain brand markets
to align themselves with their competitors. Take cosmetics for
example, in fact most luxury goods, use white space in their
marketing material to 'tell' the reader that they are sophisticated,
of high quality and generally expensive. The opposite can be said
of most Direct Mail you get through your letterbox; Red, white and
black, bold typography and very little whitespace. The result is a
down-market impression.

Take the following example.

Less space = cheap   *White space = luxury*

The content is the same on both designs, as are the elements such
as photography. The design elements differ however, to create two
designs which are at opposite ends of the brand spectrum.

Of course, this is a very simplified view of the world and there's a
lot more that goes into brand recognition than simply White Space.
But what I'm trying to get at is if a brief lands on your desk for a
luxury brand, I'll bet the client and audience of that product expects
white space in their marketing material and plenty of it to align it
with their competitors.

Active and Passive White Space

White Space is often used to create a balanced, harmonious layout. One that just 'feels' right. It can also be used to take the reader on a journey through the design. In the same way a photographer leaves 'looking room' in a portrait shot, by positioning the subject off the centre of the frame and having them looking into the remaining space, a designer can do this to increase the effectiveness of their design.

Another way of looking at white space is by how a reader, or user, reacts to it. White space can not only be used by the designer to create harmony and balance in design, or to help position a brand, but it can be used to lead a reader from one element to another. This is called Active White Space.

Let's take the following example before any active white space is applied:

Ponting defends England hierarchy

Triumphant Australia captain Ricky Ponting believes the level of criticism aimed at England coach Duncan Fletcher and captain Andrew Flintoff is unfair.
Australia won the first three Tests to regain the Ashes, and have won 14 out of 15 overall since their loss in 2005.
"There are 11 guys in the team, or 13 in the squad, and its very harsh to blame the coach and captain" he siad.
"They havent played anywhere near as well as they'd liked but we havent given them the opportunity to"
Ponting is only to well aware of the emotions that Fletchat and Flintoff are experiencing, as it is only 15 months since he became the first Australia captain for 19 years to lose an Ashes series. Ponting, who celebrated his 32nd birthday on Tuesday, has responded magnificently with the bat in the current series, making over 500 runs in his first six innings, including two big centuries.

So, everything is pretty cramped here. We then need to add some white space to create the harmony and visual comfort in the design. Here, I'm adding margins, changing the type family and weight and also adding some leading, (or line–height as it's also known).

Ponting defends England hierarchy

Triumphant Australia captain Ricky Ponting believes the level of criticism aimed at England coach
Duncan Fletcher and captain Andrew Flintoff is unfair.

Australia won the first three Tests to regain the Ashes, and have won 14 out of 15 overall since their
loss in 2005.

"There are 11 guys in the team, or 13 in the squad, and its very harsh to blame the coach and
captain" he siad.

"They havent played anywhere near as well as they'd liked but we havent given them the
opportunity to"

Ponting is only to well aware of the emotions that Fletchat and Flintoff are experiencing, as it is only
15 months since he became the first Australia captain for 19 years to lose an Ashes series.

Ponting, who celebrated his 32nd birthday on Tuesday, has responded magnificently with the bat in
the current series, making over 500 runs in his first six innings,
including two big centuries.

The white space that has been added here is Passive White Space.
There is a theory that Passive White Space is white space that is
present within a composition that is unconsidered. I disagree: that's
just bad design. Passive Whitespace still has an important job to
do; it's there to create breathing room and balance. Now, within
this content is something that I want the reader to see, the second
quote. I could highlight it with a different colour or make the type
size larger. I could do all of those at the same time. In this instance
however, I've added white space around the element to draw the
users eye, in addition to reducing the white space of the type, not
the tracking, but actually making the type bold. This is Active
White Space. White Space that is added to a composition to better
emphasise or structure information.

Ponting defends England hierarchy

Triumphant Australia captain Ricky Ponting believes the level of criticism aimed at England coach
Duncan Fletcher and captain Andrew Flintoff is unfair.

Australia won the first three Tests to regain the Ashes, and have won 14 out of 15 overall since their
loss in 2005.

"There are 11 guys in the team, or 13 in the squad, and its very harsh to blame the coach and
captain" he siad.

**"They havent played anywhere near as well as they'd liked but we havent given them the
opportunity to"**

Ponting is only to well aware of the emotions that Fletchat and Flintoff are experiencing, as it is only
15 months since he became the first Australia captain for 19 years to lose an Ashes series.

Ponting, who celebrated his 32nd birthday on Tuesday, has responded magnificently with the bat in
the current series, making over 500 runs in his first six innings, including two big centuries.

Practice, practice, practice

Sometimes, the only way to get to grips with a concept that can be as arbitrary and subjective as White Space, is to practice. In the same way martial artists have to spend hours upon hours of drilling simple techniques, graphic designers have to do the same. For many designers, this part of the craft is all but forgotten once you leave High School and replaced with classes on lateral thinking and design history. Working under the pressure of real clients demanding real work leaves little room for the time needed for these design 'drills'. If you do find yourself with a spare hour or two though, I have a great place to start.

Graphic design students have conducted these types of compositional exercises for decades and luckily for us, some of the design legends of past years have documented the process. One of my favourites has to be Emil Ruder.

Emil Ruder was a Swiss typographer who died in 1970. After 21 years of teaching typography, he produced a book called 'Typography: A Design Manual' (ISBN: 3-7212-0043-8).

'The book is deliberately restricted to pure typography, to working with prefabricated types which are subordinated to a precise system of measurements. Its purpose is to make apparent the laws of typography and – in spite of certain common features - the contrast between it and graphic design which in both the selection and means of their application, is freer and more complex.'

So, in that sense, Ruder's teachings are fairly black and white. There is a focus on typography and the subtlety of designing with letterforms. Ruder takes you through the rights and wrongs, which is a great place to start learning the fundamental principles. There are some great exercises in there covering not only white space, but also other compositional devices. It's chock–a–block with drills. It's expensive, but I urge you to buy this book and follow the examples.

White Space is not about the space in between things; the space 'left over'. Knowing how to design and manipulate the space outside, in and around your content will not only give your readers a head start, or your product the right market positioning, but will perhaps make you see your content in a new light.

Chapter Twenty–Three
Grid Systems

Before we even begin to tackle designing grid systems we need to have a basic understanding of what they are, why we use them and where they came from.

In the context of graphic design, a grid is an instrument for ordering graphical elements of text and images. The grid is a child of Constructivist art and came into being through the same thought processes that gave rise to that art movement. Clear links can also be drawn between the Concrete–Geometrical art of the Zurich school in the 1930's and several notable artists of this movement made important contributions to typography through their fine art.

It was around this period that the grid system moved from the domain of art and into one of typography and commercial design.

First of all when talking about grid systems we have to mentally separate form and function. We have to think about aesthetics and proportions as a result of considered construction. This can be quite tricky for designers who have been schooled in the 'you'll know it's right when it feels right' school of composition. But as you read earlier in this part, 'feeling right' is an emotional reaction to construction, to mathematics.

Ratios and equations are everywhere in grid system design, such as my example from the chapter on the Rule of Thirds. Relational measurements are what define most systems, from simple leaflet design to the complexity of newspaper grids. To design a successful grid system you have to become familiar with these ratios and proportions, from rational, whole–number ratios such as 1:2, 2:3, 3:4 and those irrational proportions based on the construction of circles, such as the Golden Section 1:1.618 or the standard DIN sizes 1:1.4146.

These ratios are ubiquitous in modern society, from the buildings around us to patterns in nature. Using these ratios successfully in a grid system can be the deciding factor in whether or not a design, not only functions, but has aesthetic appeal too.

A grid system is a grid design that has been designed in such a way that it can be applied to several different uses without altering its form. An example of this would be a grid system for a book whereby you have many different page types – part-opening, title, half-title etc. – and would need only one grid to use on all the page types. Or a website that has a homepage, a section index, a category index, and an article page. A grid system provides consistency across these pages or sections.

The danger with designing a system to cope with many different variants is complexity. When you add complexity, you can decrease usability and there is a danger the grid would become so complex the designer can't use it. This thought should always be running through your head when designing a grid system – keep it simple, but comprehensive, and above all, usable.

It is often said of grid systems that they limit the scope for creativity or leave no freedom. Karl Gerstner, one of Switzerland's pre-eminent graphic designers, was aware of this conflict with the designer's adoption of grid systems.

'The typographic grid is a proportional regulator for type-matter, tables, pictures and so on. It is a priority programme for a content as yet unknown. The difficulty lies in finding the balance between maximum formality and maximum freedom, or in other words, the greatest number of constant factors combined with the greatest possible variability.'

The grid is a regulatory system that pre-empts the basic formal decisions in the design process. Its preconditions help in the structuring, division and ordering of content. I'm not saying a well-designed grid will solve all of your compositional problems, far from it, but it goes some way to creating a coherent structure in design that in turn creates the aesthetic values all of us are seeking in our designs.

Constructing a Grid System

The canvas for a grid system is determined by the media size; a book, magazine, signage, or a website. The benefit for designing in more traditional media forms is that your canvas will remain constant. It will not change its shape. Of course on the web, the user can not only view your site in many different browsers, on multiple platforms, but can also resize their browser window to the resolution of their screen. Designing to such variables is a challenge. To successfully design a grid system for the modern web, we have to look at a best-case scenario, and graceful degradation.

In 2006, Jakob Nielsen wrote on his famous Alertbox:

'Optimise web pages for 1024 x 768 pixels'

Then, 60% of all monitors were set at 1024 x 768 pixels. Now, in 2009, that number is down to 30%, with the majority of monitors shipping with higher resolutions. 800 x 600 px resolution is hovering somewhere in the region of 5%.

If we use 1024px as the base, that means we will be accommodating over 90% of users. Many of our users will be using higher resolutions, so we have to take that into account also.

The Brief

Any grid system design will begin with a brief. With that brief will come constraints. What I look for in a brief is a fixed element from which to derive the grid. That element could be the screen resolution, (as best we can estimate), or it could be something as simple as image sizes.

For example, if you were redesigning a site and the site owner had a huge amount of images that he still required in the new site, I'd start by looking at the horizontal size of the images, and seeing if I could subdivide to create by unit size. If the images were 240px wide, you could divide them by 4, to give 60px, then use 10px of that for your gutter, giving you a unit size of 50px. Extrapolating that value out would give you a grid of 16 columns of a 50px unit, with a 10px gutter. The beauty of this approach is that you can be sure that the fixed part of the brief – the constraint – can be accommodated with ease.

Ratios

Ratios are at the core of any well-designed grid system.
Sometimes those ratios are rational, such as 1:2 or 2:3, others
are irrational such as the 1:1.414, (the proportion of A4 paper).
As I discussed earlier in this Part, you can use the Rule of Thirds
to create a grid system, or the Golden Section to create more
complex grid structures. The challenge is using these ratios
in a way that will help you create more balanced, harmonious
compositions.

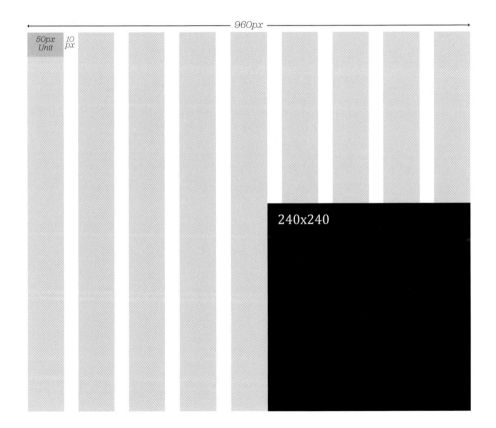

Grid Anatomy

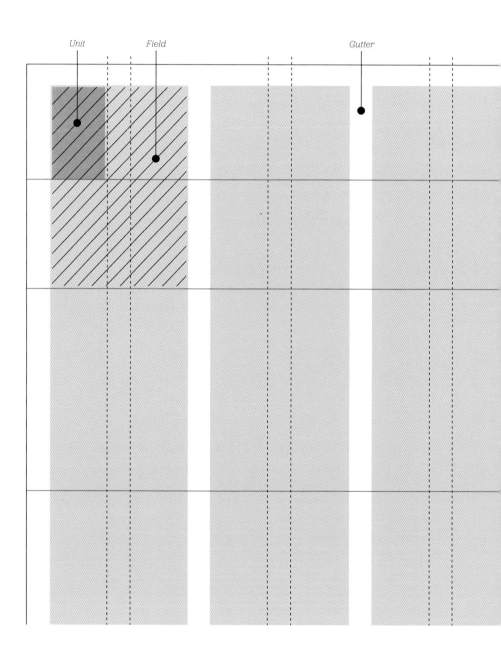

Margin

Hanging Line

Hanging Line

Hanging Line

Relational units

At the heart of every grid is the unit. The unit is a base piece from which the rest of the grid is derived. As discussed in the previous example, the unit can be derived from constraints such as the content elements you have to work with, or it can be derived from the maximum screen resolution you are designing to.

When designing for books, or other printed material, the unit is normally derived from the typeface size. So, if you are setting 12pt type, the unit of the grid is 12pt, or a multiple of 12. There is a relationship between the layout and the size of the typeface. Em-based, or 'elastic' layouts make this possible on the web.

If you are setting your type at 1em – the default in most browsers for this is 16px – then your unit size could also be derived from this measurement.

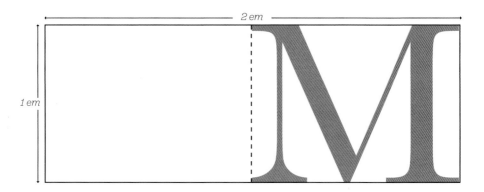

By doing this, you are creating a relationship between your typography, and your layout. They will be tied together. The grid created from the unit will be related to type size. Any layout created on this grid – any element placed within the composition – will be harmoniously connected. And, as the user resizes their text, the composition and layout can be retained. The relationship isn't lost.

Creating grids in Photoshop or on paper is one thing, making them work in a browser, across multiple browsers and operating systems is another. To help us achieve this, you can use a CSS framework.

Using CSS Frameworks

CSS frameworks can help make building your grid easier. They can ensure that potentially complex layouts render correctly on, ahem, difficult browsers – yes, I'm looking at you IE 6!

As defined by Wikipedia, a CSS framework is:

> 'A CSS framework is a library that is meant to allow for easier, more standards-compliant styling of a webpage using the Cascading Style Sheets language. Just like programming and scripting languages, CSS frameworks package a number of ready-made options for designing and outlaying a webpage.'

Which all sounds good. The aim of a CSS framework is to take away some of those repetitive tasks, whilst remaining confident your site won't break if you build another layout.

There are a number of frameworks you can download, ranging from the complex, (such as the Yahoo! UI Library grid framework), to the simple 960.gs. I'm going to talk about one framework here – Blueprint – and specifically how to use it as a basis for your grid layout.

Blueprint

Available at *http://www.blueprintcss.com*

The theory behind Blueprint started life in the minds of a few great designers and developers at The World Company, a news media company, in the US. Jeff Croft, together with Nathan Borror and Christian Metts devised a CSS framework for the website LJWorld.com. Jeff wrote an article about it on A List Apart, and Olav Bjorkoy made the theory real, and Blueprint was born.

Blueprint does the following things:

· Resets standard browser behaviour.
· Applies a sensible typographic stylesheet.
· Provides a flexible grid stylesheet.
· Has a basic, but serviceable, print stylesheet.
· Is tested, and works in, IE 6.

All of these styles can be overridden of course. Specifically, it's important to point out that the grid.css can be customised by way of the extremely handy Grid Generator.

Grid generator: *http://kematzy.com/blueprint-generator/*

This allows you to break out of the cookie-cutter approach of the 950px grid. Not every site we design will start from this base measurement or the web would look like a very boring place. Make sure you design your grid first, and then use this generator to create the Blueprint grid.css file for you.

Blueprint ships with a plugin architecture. To add elements, such as icons or tabs, simply create a new stylesheet in the plugin directory to hook in your new styles.

Blueprint is a large framework, and has been criticised for making you add non-semantic class names in your HTML, like 'span-8'. The main point of criticism is that these are presentational class names, indicating how a column in a grid will look. Good web standards HTML requires you to add class names with semantic value, like 'navigation', 'content', or 'sub-content'. Well, you can add semantic value to a Blueprint layout by including them as well. For example:

```
<div class="navigation span-24">
     Your navigation
</div>
```

Alternatively, you can add the semantic value to the ID of the div.

```
<div id="navigation" class="span-24">
     Your navigation
</div>
```

Using Blueprint, you will end up with more HTML markup in your document. You will have more divs, with more class names and IDs. If you can live with that, and if Blueprint helps you create great, flexible layouts, then I think that's fine.

Drupal.org – a redesign process using Blueprint

I've seen great value in Blueprint when using it for rapid prototyping. Specifically, Mark Boulton Design, the small design studio I run, used Blueprint to build the prototypes for the redesign of Drupal.org.

The process for the redesign of Drupal.org was a twelve week exercise. We released weekly prototype designs based on information architecture, user testing and feedback, community feedback, and revised business goals. With such tight timeframes, we needed to focus on the user experience and design of the site, rather than worrying about fixing IE 6 bugs. We needed a CSS framework.

We started out using Blueprint to create quick lo fi HTML prototypes. These were essentially wireframes created using the various classes and styles available with Blueprint. As time went on, we needed to create more and more plugins for Blueprint for things like tabs, buttons, tables etc.

When the prototype reached a certain point – iteration 6 – we needed to start applying a visual design to the completed wireframes. This is where Blueprint came into its own. With minimal changes to the HTML documents, we were able to add a Drupal.css stylesheet to override a lot of the default styles and start to apply a Drupal design. Through the iterative process, we were able to build upon this to produce quite different looking designs from release to release. All the while, the Blueprint core css files remained the same. That way, we could ensure that if we needed to upgrade Blueprint for whatever reason, we'd be able to do so without breaking the site.

The final version of the redesigned Drupal.org, in all likelihood, will not use Blueprint as its CSS framework. Whilst the various templates look great, the HTML in the background is bloated, and could be dramatically improved. If you plan on using Blueprint for a production environment, or on a live site, make sure that you pay particular attention to this. Make sure you keep your HTML nice and trim.

Drupal™

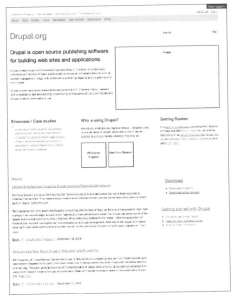

Left: **Drupal.org** wireframes
created using **Blueprint**

Right: **Drupal.org** redesign

Chapter Twenty–Four
Breaking the grid

One of the biggest complaints from designers that I've heard in relation to grid–based design is that they can limit your creativity.

I don't agree, actually, but I can see how that viewpoint has arisen. Sticking to a rigid grid can seem stifling when compared to a free, creative, fluid design process many designers are comfortable with. At times, designing using a grid can feel more like mathematics or engineering. As designers, it's our natural inclination to want to do things differently. Not to conform. And you know what? That's okay. It's okay to break free of the grid every now and then. In fact, I'd encourage it.

Should Everything Always Line Up?

Before CSS was widely adopted by the browser manufacturers as a good thing, web designers used HTML tables to layout their web pages. At the time, this was good. It allowed web designers to create layouts in a visual language they understood – columns, rows, gutters, (or padding), and margins. But, we all know now that tables for layouts are a bad thing. Now, we use CSS to lay out our web sites. We can still use the same terminology to create our columns and rows, our gutters and margins. The only difference is, we're using different HTML markup in the background. Of course, CSS uses the 'box model' to render the various elements such as padding, margins and content. This is good as well – boxes fit well into our columns.

But what happens when we want to break free of those boxes? Why would you want to do that?

Grid systems provide answers to compositional problems. They're there to help. But sometimes, it's useful – no, crucial – that we break free of the grid to provide emphasis, importance, visual interest, or increased usability. Sometimes breaking free of the grid is exactly the thing you should be doing. The trick is, knowing when to do it.

Breaking your own rules

First thing to remember is that this is your grid system. You designed it to help you with a layout. It shouldn't be a rigid tool that you can't change. There are many times when I'm halfway through a project, for whatever reason, i realise that the grid system is not helping me. Either there is not enough flexibility in the columns, or I failed to grasp the complexity of the constraints of the project. Both of these things necessitate tweaking your grid system, or, in some cases, going back to the drawing board.

And, you know what? That's just fine. Don't beat yourself up about it. Projects are fluid, and things sometimes don't work out. So, change them.

Content Out

Designing grids for print publications is similar to designing grids for the web. For newspapers, the grid design is abstracted from the content – a designer doesn't know day-to-day what content is going to populate the grid. Instead of guessing, a designer needs to establish what content 'types' will populate the grid. These can range from simple lists, headings, and paragraphs through to more complex tables and illustrations.

Finding patterns

On the web, most of the time, we don't know what the content will be that will inhabit our templates. However, we can make a pretty good estimation as to what the content types will be. If we're redesigning an existing site, and repurposing existing content, we can look through that content to try to establish patterns. This is called a Content Audit, and is usually conducted by an Information Architect, or a site editor. Whilst useful, the content audit focuses solely on content, rather than content types or patterns. It's a designer's job to delve into this content and try and establish the patterns.

For a new design, the job is somewhat easier and less laborious. By talking it through with the client, you can establish the types of content they need on the new site. Testing or interviewing users will also help massively in giving an indication of what type of content you should be designing.

The web is already full of design patterns and conventions for particular content types. For lists, through to comment forms, and registration processes. The web is maturing to the point where we don't need to rethink these patterns from the ground up every time we start a new project. This is where continued research, and being actively involved in the web – both as a professional, and a 'consumer' – can really pay dividends. By continually looking at the web, and by using the web, you become familiar with the patterns – you start to see them everywhere.

Designing to worse case scenario

I try and adopt this approach on every design project I undertake. I try and design to the worse case scenario. What happens if the user increases the font size by 200%? What happens if the editor of the site uploads the wrong size image? What happens if an administrator of the site chooses the wrong template for that section? With all of the questions, how can you be sure your design will stand up to it? This is the modern web. Things can 'break' very easily. That crafted design is only moments away from looking a complete disaster unless you take steps to protect it.

You may have heard the term 'graceful degradation' in web design. That, and 'progressive enhancement'. The former ensures that sites degrade gracefully in older browsers, but also when other factors influence the presentation such as the user increasing the font size, or Javascript being turned off. The latter describes the use of technology – be it CSS, or Javascript – to take advantage of newer browsers. Well, you can take the same approach when designing the fundamentals of your grid systems. Make sure that when viewed on older browsers, your grid system adapts, ensuring the content is still readable. Ensure that when using newer browsers, you take advantage of new technology available to you – for example, the new tags in HTML 5, such as `<header>`, or `<footer>`.

Less, not more

It's easy on any project to bite off more than you can chew. Auditing a site for a redesign may throw up over twenty different content types, all of which have to be designed, built, and accommodated into a flexible grid system. It's a considerable undertaking. So, start off small.

I like to start off any design with establishing the core typographic content types. These are:

- Headings
- Paragraphs
- Lists (unordered and ordered)
- Tables

That's it, just four typographic content types. These will form the basis of probably 80% of your content – in one form or another.

Emphasising content

Emphasis can be given to content in a variety of ways, many
of which I've talked about in this book. But, when using a grid
system, one of the best ways to draw the user's eye, is by NOT
placing that element on the grid. A loose placement on the grid,
either by nudging an element this way or that, will make it stand
out against its strictly aligned neighbours. Use an image on an
angle, or nudge navigation 10% higher.

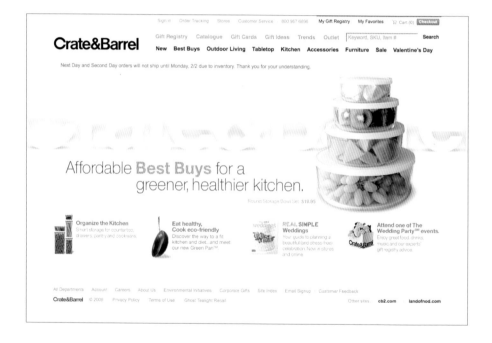

The Crate and Barrel website is a fine example of grid-based
design. The under–pinning grid structure provides a skeleton
upon which the visual elements of the website are arranged. The
grid provides unity between sections:

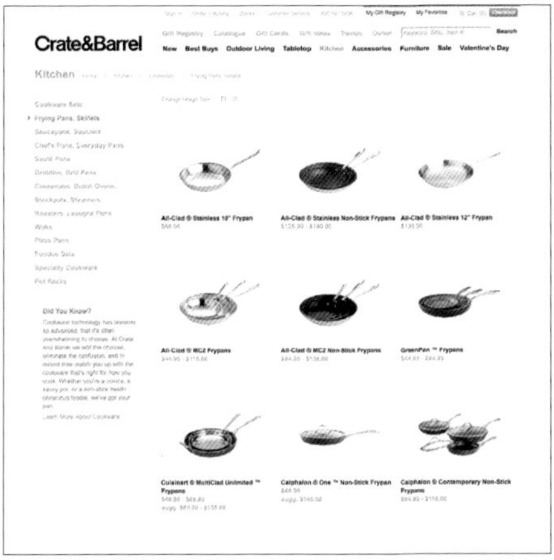
Crate&Barrel
New Best Buys Outdoor Living Tabletop Kitchen Accessories Furniture Sale Valentine's Day
Kitchen
All-Clad ® Stainless 10" Frypan
All-Clad ® Stainless Non-Stick Frypans
All-Clad ® Stainless 12" Frypan
All-Clad ® MC2 Frypans
All-Clad ® MC2 Non-Stick Frypans
GreenPan ™ Frypans
Cuisinart ® MultiClad Unlimited ™ Frypans
Calphalon ® One ™ Non-Stick Frypan
Calphalon ® Contemporary Non-Stick Frypans
Did You Know?

Crate&Barrel
New Best Buys Outdoor Living Tabletop Kitchen Accessories Furniture Sale Valentine's Day
Kitchen
Cookware Sets
Frying Pans, Skillets
Saucepans, Sauciers
Chef's Pans, Everyday Pans
Sauté Pans
Griddles, Grill Pans
Casseroles, Dutch Ovens
Stockpots, Steamers
Roasters, Lasagna Pans
Woks
Pizza Pans
Fondue Sets
Calphalon ® Tri-Ply Copper Cookware with Bonus Frypan and Bonus Braiser Set
Did You Know?
New Reduced Standard Delivery Rates

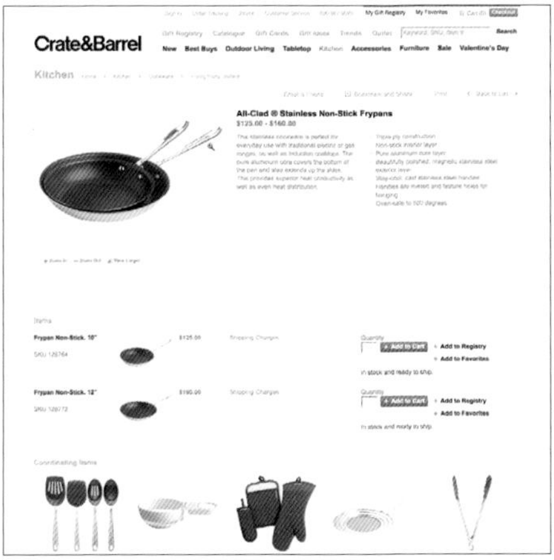
Crate&Barrel
New Best Buys Outdoor Living Tabletop Kitchen Accessories Furniture Sale Valentine's Day
Kitchen
All-Clad ® Stainless Non-Stick Frypans
$125.00 - $160.00
Frypan Non-Stick, 10"
Frypan Non-Stick, 12"
Add to Registry
Add to Favorites

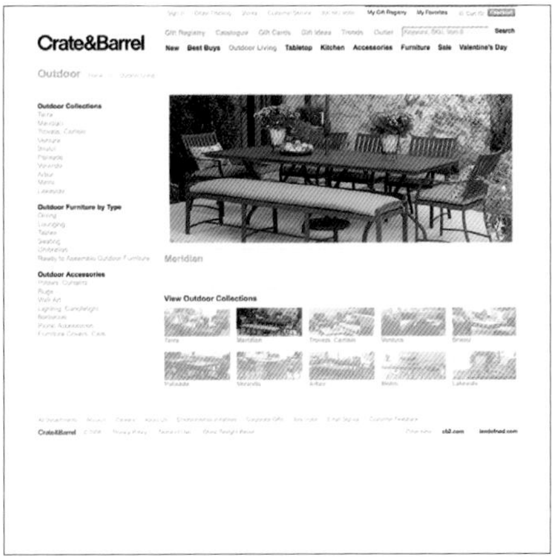
Crate&Barrel
New Best Buys Outdoor Living Tabletop Kitchen Accessories Furniture Sale Valentine's Day
Outdoor
Outdoor Collections
Outdoor Furniture by Type
Outdoor Accessories
Meridian
View Outdoor Collections

However, strict adherence to a grid comes with some pit-falls and I believe Crate and Barrel has inadvertently fallen down one of these pits.

The site has a calm, even appearance. No doubt, this is by design. But the design has an even appearance that makes drawing attention to any content, button, product, or widget difficult. You can understand the designers wanting to draw attention to the product photography through a simple, clear design. But, with some simple changes of position, we can provide some much-needed emphasis to certain page elements.

The emphasis, on this occasion, is provided by NOT aligning a content element to the underlying grid. The content element is moved slightly off the line – and the amount is up to you, there is no magic formula for this. It's just enough to show that this element is different, it's special or important, and we want the user to see it as soon as possible.

Breaking the grid does require an understanding of how a grid is constructed. Just like a building, if you remove, or break some of the load-bearing structure, a grid system will fall apart. If you've designed a grid, and part way through the layout process, things just aren't working out – maybe you're having to create extra columns, or change the size of the unit – that's fine. Don't see the grid as a structure that, once created, cannot be changed, revised or thrown out completely.

Product page. The title and product description are uncomfortably aligned to the grid.

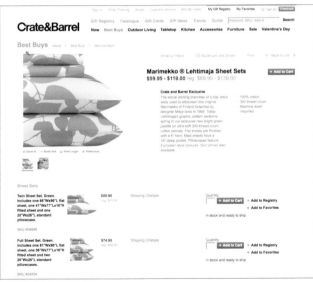

For my version, I keep the title and price aligned, but increase the size and move the description off the grid and align it with the list of links above.

It's a subtle, but effective change. The resultant whitespace around the title is now giving emphasis.

Chapter Twenty–Five
Bringing it all together:
De Standaard

De Standaard

In June 2008, a team from De Standaard
– www.standaard.be – approached my
design studio with a request to see if we'd
be interested in redesigning their website.

De Standaard is a Flemish daily newspaper published in Belgium
with a circulation of over 100,000. It is a high quality newspaper
with an interesting history spanning eighty years – through Nazi
occupation of Belgium, to political unrest, through to bankruptcy.

This case study is somewhat of an exclusive for this book at the
time of publication. The new De Standaard site was relaunched
in Q1 2009.

De Standaard

« ARCHIEF   DINSDAG 17 JUNI, 2008

ANA IVANOVIC IS VOOR HET EERST NUMMER 1
Op de vandaag gepubliceerde wereldranglijst van het vrouwentennis staat de Servische Ana Ivanovic voor ...

NIEUWS   OPINIES   LIFESTYLE   ONTSPANNING   IN BEELD

🔒 VOOR ONZE ABONNEES

Meest recent   Binnenland   Buitenland   Economie .BIZ   Cultuur   Media   Sport   Wetenschap   Beroemd&bizar

TELEX: 'Tegenbod op Innogenetics

Zoek

Wereld kijkt ongerust naar Zimbabwe ★ 129

LOCATION – Cras quis lorem. Pellentesque condimentum neque et nisi. Cras nec tellus quis sapien ultricies dictum. Phasellus a nunc. Mauris pellentesque porta pede. Duis at arcu. Donec vitae erat lacinia orci luctus tempus. Nullam fringilla semper orci. Duis blandit molestie libero. Sed sem ipsum, imperdiet et, congue a, varius nec, ante.

Quisque bibendum aliquam nulla. Fusce nec justo quis tellus lacinia molestie.

Article: Ut id ante in neque porttitor cursus.
Article: Vivamus a nisl in nulla pretium bibendum. Mauris diam nisi, vestibulum id
Dossier: Donec et augue mollis nulla vehicula dapibus
Debate: Lorem ipsum dolor sit amet, consectetuer adipiscing elit.   1681 reacties

VIDEO

FOTO

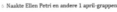

'Geen sprake van impasse' ★ 43

BRUSSEL – Premier Yves Leterme (CD&V) ontkent dat er sprake is van een impasse. 'De onderhandelingen zijn niet geblokkeerd. Er is zelfs enige vooruitgang merkbaar', zei hij vandaag na afloop van de ministerraad.

Video: title of video clip   *Photo:* Image gallery link   title of related article that can be quite long

Rudy Demotte breidt faciliteiten Wallonië uit ★ 82

Waals minister-president Rudy Demotte (PS) wil financiële steun verlenen aan gemeenten in zijn gewest die faciliteiten verlenen aan anderstaligen. Vanaf 15 september wordt een proefproject opgestart.

Photo: Image gallery link   title of related article that can be quite long

Levenslang voor Ait Oud

Abdallah Ait-Oud is veroordeeld tot levenslange opsluiting en 10 jaar ter ....
MORE »

STANDAARD.BIZ

Index	Verschi (%)
BEL20	▾ – 1.63
EURONEXT100	▾ – 1.63
CAC40	▾ – 1.63
AEX	▾ – 1.63
FRANKFURT	▾ – 1.63
NASDAQ 100	▾ – 1.63
DOW JONES	▾ – 1.63

VIDEO

Kleren, geen seks

Gecrashte Boeing vervoerde geen wapens

Bureaustoelen, armleuningen, uniformen en wagens: dat is de hoofdmoot van de lading van

'Abortus bij medische afwijking kan niet'

De koepel van de christelijke ziekenhuizen heeft een advies verstuurd naar haar instellin-

The Brief

The first meeting took place in the National Portrait Gallery in London on a nice sunny day. Immediately I was struck by the lofty goals of the redesign of the website. The New York Times website, together with The Times in the UK, and The Guardian, were all mentioned as the benchmark that needed to be set for the design. The bar was indeed set high.

It was important, during that initial briefing session, that I understood the motivations behind the need to redesign. They can be summarised as:

· Improve the core content
· Improve the brand and appeal to the users of the website, not the readers of the paper
· Improve the innovation of the new site
· Improve the business model (better ad positioning, sell subscriptions, cross promotion)
· Outdated look and feel.
· Integration of new content management system.

As you can see, the breadth of the design problem was considerable. From the business strategy and revenue models, all the way up to the typography and brand perception. All of it had to be considered, rationalised, researched, and designed.

Should a newspaper online look offline?

During the research and discovery phase of the project, I kept asking myself the same questions regarding newspapers online. Do they need to look like their offline siblings? Should I try to be emulating some of the conventions used in the physical newspaper?

It's an important consideration, and something I'm not alone in contemplating. Information Architects, (iA), the small design studio in Japan, wrote a seminal document called 'The Future of News', where they highlighted the risks and opportunities for newspaper companies in the coming years to take advantage of the web. Many of these were relevant for this project.

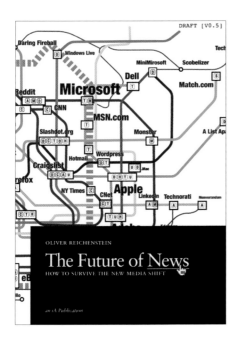

Front cover, back page and 1 page spread from the **Future of News document** by Oliver Reichenstein

ENTER

News organisations cannot continue to ignore the global shift from institutionally controlled media to user controlled media. They have to redefine their processes and face the obvious question: Do we still need old media for news?

»A good newspaper is a country speaking to itself.«[1] These are not the words of Internet junkie high on Web 2.0. This is ARTHUR MILLER, defining newspapers back in 1961. If Miller is right about news being a conversation,[2] the obvious *instrument for organizing this conversation is the Web*. It is fast, it is versatile and it is conversational in its nature.

There are obvious signs that the shift in the usage of media is irreversible. While the access statistics of social media sites are going through the roof, newspapers loose readers online and offline. Young people read more but read less printed materials. Ad revenue prognostics for the Internet point to stupefying future while all other media are feeling the pressure already. In a special edition on the decline of printed news The Economist stated that »the most useful bit

1 THE ECONOMIST, Aug 24th 2006 http://www.economist.com/opinion/displaystory.cfm?story_id=7830218
2 Reminding us of "markets as conversation", as coined by THE CLUETRAIN MANIFESTO, http://www.cluetrain.com/

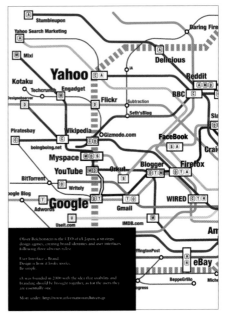

iA highlighted the following of threats to not migrating to
the web:

1 **'Lower reading experience.'**
Printed newspapers are easy to read. On the train, the
underground, on the way to work. The web isn't.

2 **'Losing journalistic quality.'**

3 **'Severing cultural roots.'**
The printed word has a rich, important heritage.

However, the opportunities, in my mind, far outweigh
the threats.

1 **'Optimised reading experience'.**
Given the immediacy of news content, having relevant supportive
content – in the form of text, image, video and multimedia –
enriches the reading experience.

2 **'Improved democracy'.**
The user can have their say. And, in a 'web 2' world, that is
actively encouraged. It was a key component of De Standaard
redesign that the user engagement was an integral part of any
redesign, not just an add-on.

3 **'Historic development'.**
Newspapers will eventually migrate to the web, and printed
newspapers will be a luxury. We're already seeing this with a
steady decline in newspaper circulation.

These threats and opportunities underpin the design strategy
for the new site. How could I lower the risks, and exploit the
opportunities in the design system we produced?

The Constraints

All projects have constraints. Without them, designing would be incredibly difficult. However frustrating they can be, they are our boundaries; a framework in which to work. And typically, De Standaard had plenty of them.

Existing content

www.standaard.be had been around for years. During that time, there had been attempts to enforce standards; from ads to image sizes. It was our job to audit as much of that content as possible, and then to define new standards that fit the patterns and trends.

Brand integration

As I mentioned, De Standaard is a newspaper with a rich history. The readership however, is typical of a once-broadsheet newspaper; older, male, white-collar. The website, however, has a slightly different audience. Still predominantly male, they are younger, less conservative in their political views, and regular consumers of the web. In that sense, the two brands are related but not the same. This subtle difference had to be accounted for in the design.

Revenue

Like most newspapers, De Standaard relies on advertising and subscriptions for its revenue.

Previously, www.standaard.be used some standard ad sizes, and some bespoke ads for running internal promotions and competitions. With so many different sizes, some standardised, and some not, any changes to design and global layout were challenging. Ads were shoe-horned in where they would fit, rather than strategic positioning.

Modular Content, Modular Grid

Newspapers, like most text-based material, are comprised of typographic elements. During the initial discovery and research phase, we conducted a number of audits on the content elements on the site.

Content objects

We were provided with a list of content object requirements as part of the project brief. These ranged from simple article lists, and teasers, to more complex video players and tv listings.

30px

277px

Promo section links
Title links to articles within the specific section.

Article teaser
Used to focus users to
articles within news.

Lorem ipsum

**Mauris viverra ipsum vesti bul
um erat. Duis et arcu et turpis
au ctor condimentum. Mauris
dig nis sim enim nec. .tortor.**

LEES MEER | LATER »

Homepage article summary
These summaries have a title,
summary, image, read more,
read later, star rating, links to
media and
related articles.

▼ 'Geen sprake van impasse'
10px

Premier Yves Leterme (CD&V)
ontkent dat er sprake is van een
impasse. 'De onderhandelingen zijn
niet geblokkeerd.

LEES MEER »   LATER +   ☆ 43

10px
▲ ▦ title of video clip
     ▨ Image gallery link
     * Title of related article that can be quite long
30px
▼

Rudy Demotte breidt faciliteiten Wallonië uit

Waals minister-president Rudy
Demotte (PS) wil financiële steun
verlenen aan gemeenten in zijn
gewest die faciliteiten verlenen.

LEES MEER »   LATER +   ☆ 82

▦ title of video clip
▨ Image gallery link
* Title of related article that can be quite long

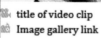

Levenslang voor Ait Oud

**Lorem ipsum dolor sit amet conse
ctetuer adipiscing elit nec tortor.**
LEES MEER »   LATER +

|←   133px   →|

Typographic elements

All written content can be structured into typographic elements; such as paragraphs, lists, headings, captions, blockquotes etc. Newspapers cover such broad stories, so from an editorial standpoint, the writers need all of the typographic elements they are used to working with. Any audit of content objects, should also incorporate an audit of the typographic elements required for the hugely varying content.

Left: **Font** and **Sizes** used for headlines and body copy.

Below: **Module Titles** and **Navigation**

Lorem ipsum
1st article title: 30px, #000000

Lorem ipsum
2nd article title: 24px, #000000

Lorem ipsum
3rd article title: 18px, #000000

Lorem ipsum dolor sit amet consectetuer adipiscing elit donec laoreet mi eu augue.
1st article summary: 17px, #333333, 19px leading

Lorem ipsum dolor sit amet consectetuer adipiscing elit donec laoreet mi eu augue.
2nd article summary: 14px, #333333, 16px leading

Lorem ipsum dolor sit amet consectetuer adipiscing elit donec laoreet mi eu augue.
3rd article summary: 13px, #333333, 15px leading

Lorem ipsum dolor sit amet consectetuer adipiscing elit donec laoreet mi eu augue.
Article body copy: 16px, #000000, 21px leading

STANDAARD.BIZ
Module titles: upper case, bold, 11px, #000000

VOOR ABONNEES
Upper case, bold, 12px, #000000

NIEUWS **OPINIES** **ECONOMIE** .BIZ
Header Navigation: Upper case, Bold, 12px, #D47F11

Meest recent   Binnenland   Buitenland   Cultuur
Header SubNavigation: Bold, 12px, #D47F11

Lead article variations

To cope with the variety of importance of lead news story items, a number of variations were explored and designed. It was also important we explored how stories can escalate. A news story can start small – breaking news – with small amounts of information and associated content such as photos and video. Over time, the story gathers more pace, more content, more exposure, and more importance. All of this has to be structured into a content object that allows the display of that flux.

We designed several versions ranging from a simple lead story, right up to the extra large version.

Wereld kijkt ongerust

De terugtrekking van oppositieleider Morgan Tsvangirai in Zimbabwe leidt tot negatieve internationale

LEES MEER » LATER » ★ 129

- title of video clip
- Image gallery link
- Title of related article that can be quite long

Lead Story
Small – Half width article.

Betancourt na zes jaar bevrijd uit jungle

Ingrid Betancourt is woensdagmiddag samen met elf Colombiaanse ex-gijzelaars aangekomen op de militaire luchthaven van Bogota. Het Colombiaanse leger redde de Frans-Colombiaanse politica, drie Amerikanen en elf andere gijzelaars uit de handen van de linkse rebellenbeweging FARC.

LEES MEER » LATER » ★ 129

- Al 40 reacties reageer zelf
- title of video clip
- Image gallery link
- Title of related article that can be quite long

Image caption that can be quite long if need be

Medium – Full width article with half width image.

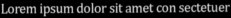

Lorem ipsum dolor sit amet con sectetuer

Sed fermentum erat vitae metus lacinia auctor. Cras convallis luctus purus. Vestibulum ante ipsum primis in faucibus orci luctus et ultrices posuere cubilia Curae mollis, risus diam ornare ante, pharetra adipiscing massa est sed ante. Aliquam lobortis eleifend ipsum.

LEES MEER » LATER » ★ 125

- Al 40 reacties reageer zelf
- Image gallery link
- Title of related article that can be quite long

Large – Full width article with full width image.

Wereld kijkt ongerust naar Zimbabwe

Sed fermentum erat vitae metus lacinia auctor. Cras convallis luctus purus. Vestibulum ante ipsum primis in faucibus orci luctus et ultrices posuere cub ili a Curae mollis, risus diam ornare ante, pharetra adipiscing massa est sed ante.

LEES MEER » LATER » ★ 129

- Al 40 reacties reageer zelf
- title of video clip
- Image gallery link
- Title of related article that can be quite long

VIDEO

FOTO

Extra Large – Full width article with full width image including video and photo thumbnails.

Several different sections with different audiences

Like most newspapers, De Standaard has daily and weekly
supplements – ranging from the popular 'Economie' business
supplement, to the 'Lifestyle' magazine. The various sections
not only needed to be accommodated in the new site, but they
also had to appeal to the different audiences. Economie, for
example, required a flexible design to incorporate the various
graphs and stock information, together with the usual editorial
content. Lifestyle required a brighter, more approachable, look.
Large photographs, multimedia galleries etc. were the order of
the day.

Both Lifestyle and '.biz' use a slightly different masthead and
logo, and different colour palettes. This reinforces the sub-
brands but also the provides orientation for the user.

Designing the Grid

The constants define the columns. De Standaard uses standard advertising units as defined by Interactive Advertising Bureau. For the new site, it was proposed the following ad units would be incorporated:

- 300 x 250 IMU – *(Medium Rectangle)*
- 728 x 90 IMU – *(Leaderboard)*

Leaderboard banner

Medium Rectangle advert

These ad units are relatively common for commercial sites, but particularly common for the newspapers. The New York Times, Guardian, and Times Online, (the three sites indicated as a benchmark for the redesign of De Standaard), all carried the Medium Rectangle, and all but the New York Times uses a Leaderboard.

In addition to these standard ad sizes, we also had to contend with existing image sizes employed by De Standaard for several years. All of this legacy content had to be included in the new design without breaking the layout.

These elements are constants. The size of these elements are fixed, and will not change over time so they are a safe starting point for us to design the grid around.

Asymmetrical columns

A lot of grids on the web are based on even numbers of grids: 12, 16, 24. On researching this project – especially by reading a huge variety of newspapers from around Europe – it became clear that actually in physical newspapers, an odd number of columns is the norm: either 5, 7, or rarely 9 columns. I believe this creates an imbalance, and therefore an opportunity to create tension in a layout. Let me explain a little.

An even number of columns is a little like using a square for composition. It's stable, balanced, and even. Using a square as a compositional base can result in a balanced layout, but the danger is the resulting design will have no movement. It's more difficult to lead the eye around a layout that has a strong symmetrical base. Think back to earlier in this part where I discussed the advantages of using a triangle as a primary compositional device.

For this reason, I opted for a five-column master for the new De Standaard grid. These columns would each be separated by a generous gutter.

These master columns then can be subdivided to give ten columns to provide more layout flexibility.

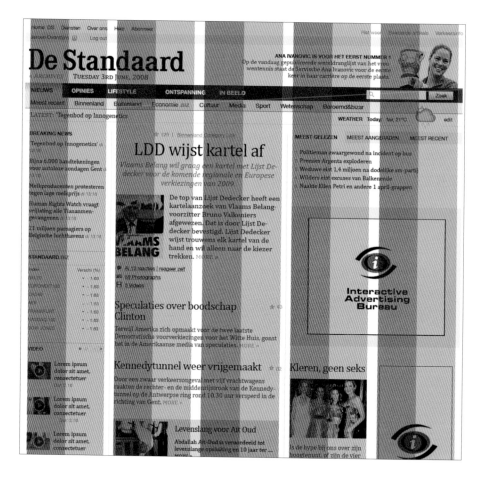

The master columns of this grid allow for a number of permutations, shown opposite.

Particularly on the initial homepage design, the five column layout allows for uneven, interesting layouts.

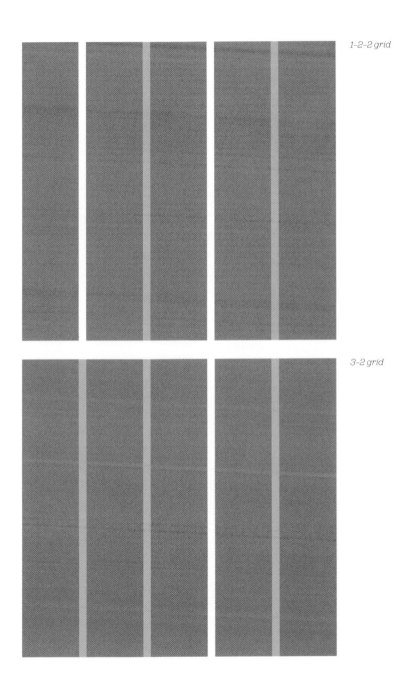

1-2-2 grid

3-2 grid

3-2 grid with design

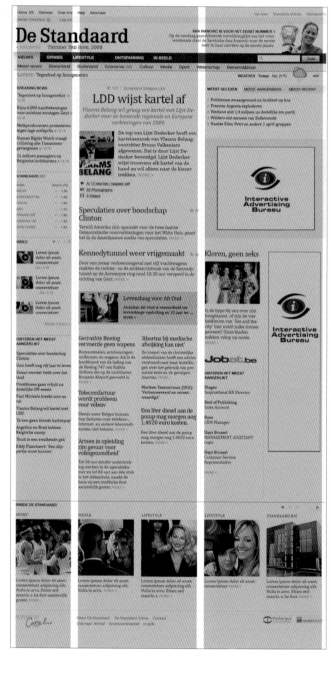

Design Exploration

Once I'd worked through the initial wireframes, and functional requirements for the various templates on the new site, I got down to some design exploration. We adopted an iterative approach to the design development. In total, there were more than ten rounds completed before we delivered the final design framework. Here's a walkthrough of the major design milestones:

The initial design direction set the typographic and colourway tone. Predominantly black and white, with a spot colour of orange.

Iteration 1

A more conventional layout was adopted for the second iteration,
with a column configuration of 3-2.

Iteration 2

This version included a completely revised masthead and main navigation bar. The previous version was too dark and visually heavy. The aim was to draw users beyond the masthead and into the content below. The previous version was acting as a visual barrier.

Iteration 3

More subtle revisions to the masthead. Incorporating orange
colour into the links creates a strong horizontal line of links. No
need for a background tone to tie all of that together.

Iteration 4

Final Homepage Iteration

Home DS   Diensten   Over ons   Help   Abonneer

De Standaard

DINSDAG 17 JUNI, 2008

ANA IVANOVIC IS VOOR HET EERST
NUMMER 1
Op de vandaag gepubliceerde
wereldranglijst van het vrouwentennis
staat de Servische Ana Ivanovic voor …

NIEUWS   OPINIES   ECONOMIE .BIZ   LIFESTYLE   ONTSPANNING   IN BEELD   **VOOR ABONNEES**

Meest recent   Binnenland   Buitenland   Cultuur   Media   Sport   Wetenschap   Beroemd en bizar

21ºC Brussels   15km Vlaanderen   - 1.63   BEL20 | Verfijn   Hallo Mark Boulton   Personaliseer | Log uit   +

Zoek

NIEUWSFLITS: Lorem ipsum dolor sit amet, consectetuer adipiscing elit. Donec purus. Vestibulum at nulla ut diam int dum accumsan. Aenean non lacus. Integer id neque id ante pulvinar facilisis. Mauris quis justo. Donec augue ante, pulvinar quis.

Wereld kijkt ongerust

De terugtrekking van oppositieleider Morgan Tsvangirai in Zimbabwe leidt tot negatieve internationale
LEES MEER »   LATER +   ☆ 129

▸ title of video clip
◫ Image gallery link
• Title of related article that can be quite long

'Geen sprake van impasse'

Premier Yves Leterme (CD&V) ontkent dat er sprake is van een impasse. 'De onderhandelingen zijn niet geblokkeerd.'
LEES MEER »   LATER +   ☆ 43

▸ title of video clip
◫ Image gallery link
• Title of related article that can be quite long

Rudy Demotte breidt faciliteiten Wallonië uit

Waals minister-president Rudy Demotte (PS) wil financiële steun verlenen aan gemeenten in zijn gewest die faciliteiten verlenen.
LEES MEER »   LATER +   ☆ 82

MEEST GELEZEN   Meest aangeraden   Meest recent

1. Politieman zwaargewond na incident op bus
2. Premies Argenta exploderen
3. Weduwe eist 1,4 miljoen na dodelijke sm-partij
4. Wilders eist excuses van Balkenende
5. Naakte Ellen Petri en andere 1 april-grappen

Win een MacBook Air internal promo big game
Doe mee!

Sterke prestaties.
Betrouwbaarheid.

STANDAARD.BIZ

Index	Verschi (%)
BEL20	▾ - 1.63
EURONEXT100	▾ - 1.63
CAC40	▾ - 1.63
AEX	▾ - 1.63
FRANKFURT	▾ - 1.63
NASDAQ 100	▾ - 1.63
DOW JONES	▾ - 1.63

VIDEO   ● ○ ○ ◂ ▸

 Lorem ipsum dolor sit amet, consectetuer
Dur: 2.16

Lorem

NIET TE MISSEN   ● ○ ○ ◂ ▸

SPORT

Lorem ipsum
Lorem ipsum dolor sit amet, consectetuer adipiscing elit.
LEES MEER »   LATER +

MEDIA

Dolor sit amet
Dolor sit amet, consectetuer adipiscing elit.
LEES MEER »   LATER +

LIFESTYLE

Consectetuer
Lorem ipsum dolor sit amet, consectetuer adipiscing elit.
LEES MEER »   LATER +

LIFESTYLE

Een perfecte week (met frisdrank)

Mark Coenen, bekend radio-man en directeur marktstrategie van de VRT, wou met zijn gezin naar Egypte. Ze wisten wat ze niet wilden, dus gingen ze op zoek op het net en vonden een bijzonder aanbod. Het werd een aparte kerstvakantie in en om Aswan, bij de Nubiërs.
LEES MEER »   LATER +

STANDAARD.BIZ

Lorem ipsum dolor sit amet, consectetuer adipiscing elit.
LEES MEER »   LATER +

 Mediargus
metriweb

 INSPIRES BY

Abonneren
Registreren
Diensten
Mail bij belangrijk nieuws
Sms bij belangrijk nieuws
De Standaard als startpagina
De Standaard Mobile

Contacteer De Standaard
Klantendienst
Redactie
Wie is wie bij De Standaard
Advertenties

Help
Sitemap
Veelgestelde vragen
Vind
Zoekertjes
Jobat
Parship

The final design as applied to the homepage and subsequent
pages throughout the site. The flexibility of the grid helped create
a coherence between sections. Shown here are the section for the
TV guide.

TV Guide

Design a system, not a website

This project had limited budget, and limited time. We didn't have the luxury of working in-house, or crafting a user experience for every single user journey on the new site. How do you approach a project of this scale, with limited resources and time? By designing a system, and not a website.

As highlighted in this chapter, we approached this project as designing a kit of parts – as a framework. A skeleton of a grid system, with modular content objects that could be placed in the grid, in various configurations, to create the site. If that approach is combined with a sensible colour palette, opportunities for art direction, and sensitive typography, as a designer, you are arming the editorial teams with all the tools they need to create a site from new and old content without designing individual pages.

We delivered the various bits and pieces together with a visual language document.

Pages from **Visual Language** document

The visual language guide documents how the site can be
built out in the future. From the various colourways for each
section, through to how the various content objects work in the
grid. It's important to note that this document is by no means a
comprehensive guide to cover every eventuality. Those types of
guideline-design documents generally fail. Many designers do
not like to work within strict constraints. Instead, we proposed
this document to be a starting point. It touches on all the different
elements of the visual language, but provides enough scope for
creative movement for the various editors and designers who will
be working on the site. Providing this framework allows people
to be creative in the future, and by doing so, they should feel a
degree of ownership. The visual language will begin to *represent
the ongoing* content on the site, not describing a designer's vision.
That is a subtle but important distinction.

The principles of layout – from composition theories to grid
systems - largely do not rely on the medium of the design's
delivery; most of the layout theories I've discussed are derived
from either print design or photography. There's a good reason
why they shouldn't be discounted.

   In 'Getting Started', I highlighted that early in the development
of web design, many designers practicing web design were print
designers. They used established conventions and graphic design
practice to create web sites. This wasn't a bad thing – it was all
they knew – but over the past ten years the words 'print' and 'web'
are often met with grimaces from web designers working in the
industry now. The old 'the web is not print' argument raises its
head every now and then, and we cover the same ground, and
reach the same conclusions. The result is that web designers are
not learning *applicable* graphic design craft. There is still much
we can learn from the practice of graphic design and layout is
just one.

Conclusion

What does it really feel like to be a designer in this industry today?

Well, let me ask you, what was the most rewarding aspect of the last project you finished? My guess is that the answers will be incredibly varied, from solving a particularly difficult interaction design problem, through to some really well constructed CSS. Modern web design is a discipline that spans a huge range of skills. Often though, the wider the span, the thinner the knowledge. That needs to change.

Graphic design has such a rich, and useful history. For example, elements of modern typography and typesetting have evolved over hundreds of years. Having at least a basic understanding of this heritage of the craft is going to arm you with some of the right tools to make a difference in your daily work.

The craft of graphic design has changed little in the past fifty years. We're still communicators. We still use colour, image, type, illustrations and layout to tell the story for our clients or customers. Language is still the vehicle for communication on the web. We still use research to inform our decisions. One of the few things that are different is the delivery medium: the web. And with that difference comes one fundamental change.

We don't control the content, the users do. The data is theirs to do with as they wish.

Graphic designers have long been in control. We take the brief from the client. We control how that message is conveyed. We control the type, the imagery and the production. We spend a long time getting it just right. Then along comes the web and gives all of that control to the user.

Suddenly, they can change the font size. They can break our carefully constructed layout. The considered whitespace goes out of the window as they move the browser window. They can choose the colours–even upload style sheets of their own. Is it any wonder so many advertising and design studios insist on using Flash and resizing the browser window to 100%. It's all about control. To control the message and delivery. The user will see this how I want them to.

I cannot understate how much of a shift that is. From schooling, right up through early career development, graphic designers rely on that constant.

Good graphic design, be it on the web, print, or broadcast, is the successful marriage of content and presentation. But, on the web, content is often abstracted from the presentation, such as being presented in an RSS reader, or content is delivered last in a project and 'plugged-in' to a template. This is one of the biggest hurdles many great designers have to get over. Embracing the web means knowing your crafted design might be viewed differently. I think this is a good thing for graphic design.

Graphic design – as I hope I've illustrated throughout this book – is much more than how something looks. Typographic design in particular pays attention to how language is structured, chunked-up, listed, and tabulated, not just the typeface choice. Web design needs to move beyond layout, fonts and colours, browser quirks, and the latest JavaScript library, and embrace the true roots of the practice: the communication of information.

And we can do plenty of that when we're out of control. By working closely with Information Architects, Writers, Developers, and Clients. By being involved in the process from day one. By paying attention to content. By art directing and trying to tell stories with our designs and interfaces. By passionately embracing the medium. And, by constantly learning.

We don't need to be completely in control to communicate. Writing a book on design for the web isn't the easiest thing to do. The web moves fast. Conventions come and go. Best practices change every six months. To write a book that is a snapshot of this flux would not only be a mistake, but actually pretty difficult. In fact, a book probably wouldn't be the best medium for that type of content.

But this little book isn't about documenting a moment in time, or providing pretty pictures of the latest trends and biggest, best designs on the web. It's about the basics of graphic design craft – the basics of communicating by design. I hope it will act both informatively and as an ongoing reference.

Now, why not go back to the beginning, and read it again. You may have missed something.

Attributions *In order of appearence*

2. Research

Definitions from http://www.reference.com || Flickr Homepage *http://www.flickr.com*

Four R Photos

Revolution - **gailf548** - *http://www.flickr.com/photos/galfred/127552283/* || Re-Expression - **Ingrid** - Ingorrr - *http://www. flickr.com/photos/ingorrr/377182375/* || Related worlds - Randy - **Randy Son Of Robert** - *http://www.flickr.com/photos/ randysonofrobert/464791157/* || Random links - **Jürgen Schiller García** - schillergarcia - *http://www.flickr.com/photos/ schillergarcia/2836059154/*

3. Typography:

Mark Boulton Design - *http://www.markboultondesign.com* || **Times Online** - *http://www.timesonline.co.uk* || **Guardian. co.uk** - *http://www.guardian.co.uk*

4. Colour

Photo of boy with camera attributed to **Nick Boulton** || **Yes Insurance** - *http://www.yesinsurance.co.uk* || **Benefit Cosmetics** - *http://www.benefitcosmetics.com* || **Coolspotters** - *http://www.coolspotters.com* || The Body Shop - *http://www. thebodyshop.co.uk* || **GHD** - *http://www.ghdhair.com/uk*

Black Photos

Life doesn't have to be Black & White - **banoootah_qtr** - *http://www.flickr.com/photos/banoootah_qtr/2781726403*
My hat is to Fabulous for my head!! - **Chris Morrow** - Hi I'm Chris... {or Birdman} - *http://www.flickr.com/photos/crush_ images/3016352014/* || Incunsueta Spello - **Alessandro Scarcella** - *http://www.flickr.com/photos/ alexscarcella/1092142727*
homeless in rotterdam || **Revi Kornmann** - *http://www.flickr.com/photos/revi/224825330* || Mar 27 05 - **mookielove** - *http://www.flickr.com/photos/mookielove/9868042/* || Eisteddfod - Attributed to **Nick Boulton**

White Photos

First Scuff!! - **.....dotted.....** - *http://www.flickr.com/photos/colourcrazy/2399790749/in/set-7215760399407985* || VW Bus-Glasgow - **David Johnson** - Manky Maxblack - *http://www.flickr.com/photos/maxblack/2668793746/* || Ice - **Marko Milošević** - Nictalopen - *http://www.flickr.com/photos/nictalopen/221960735* || People probably thought I was weird... - **.....dotted.....** - *http://www.flickr.com/photos/colourcrazy/2379003286* || grand central terminal - **Laure Padgett**-*http://www.flickr.com/photos/laurapadgett/2954855991*

Red Photos

7 Up - **Kevin Dooley** - *http://www.flickr.com/photos/pagedooley/2239200286/* || Red drum with paint - **tanakawho** - *http://www.flickr.com/photos/28481088@N00/2327920735/* || Stack - **Knut Arne Smeland** - *http://www.flickr.com/ photos/44988721@N00/229432914* || Open - **Steve Navarro** - *http://www.flickr.com/photos/snavarro/456166500* || yes, I'm feeling lucky - Tinou Bao - *http://www.flickr.com/photos/tinou/137973013* || choke when it really counts - **erin MC hammer** - *http://www.flickr.com/photos/balladist/2843633256/*

Blue Photos

Blue - **Lisa Norwood** - *http://www.flickr.com/photos/lisanorwood/1045562729* || Blue sixteen - **piermario** - *http://www.flickr.com/photos/piermario/2104143438* || Blue Lego - **JC i Núria** - *http://www.flickr.com/photos/ nuriaijoancarles/2866493684* || can you push me - **Ryan** - pimpexposure - *http://www.flickr.com/photos/ shiznotty/3032867052* || 0 GB - **Mike** - SqueakyMarmot - *http://www.flickr.com/photos/squeakymarmot/399925350*

Yellow Photos

Yellow Cab - **Seamus Murray** - *http://www.flickr.com/photos/seamusnyc/486999643* ‖ Yellow for feet - **Joe Seggiola** - *http://www.flickr.com/photos/joeseggiola/2779317752* ‖ Yellow 22 - **flattop341** - *http://www.flickr.com/photos/ flattop341/228001614* ‖ '56 Yellow bus - Jessica Merz - *http://www.flickr.com/photos/jessicafm/176739416* ‖ Perú > Lima - **antifluor** - *http://www.flickr.com/photos/antifluor/2074560932* ‖ Yellow - **wonderferret** - *http://www.flickr.com/photos/ wonderferret/1169897941*

Green Photos

Green curves - **tanakawho** - *http://www.flickr.com/photos/28481088@N00/2589282065* ‖ green banana - **Mauren Veras** - *http://www.flickr.com/photos/mauren/2322667800* ‖ Green Leaf - **Christopher Woo** - *http://www.flickr.com/photos/ deks/2209559360* ‖ Green Study 3 - **Wrote** - *http://www.flickr.com/photos/wrote/1452627659*
Hannah's green Converse - **Benny Mazur** - benimoto - *http://www.flickr.com/photos/benimoto/505273689/sizes/o* ‖ Green Bug - **waywuwei** - *http://www.flickr.com/photos/waywuwei/2275595332*

Orange Photos

Got My Orange Crush - **flattop341** - *http://www.flickr.com/photos/flattop341/223306484* ‖ Orange Force One - **Incase Designs** - *http://www.flickr.com/photos/goincase/479050237* ‖ Numbers in the orange - **Leonid Mamchenkov** - *http:// www.flickr.com/photos/mamchenkov/517724404* ‖ Orange E on a Baby Blue Dumpster (Washington, DC) - **takomabibelot** - *http://www.flickr.com/photos/takomabibelot/3031496925* ‖ oranges... - **Junichiro Aoyama** - jam343 - *http://www.flickr. com/photos/jam343/2048123*

Brown Photos

Shroom - **Jesse Kruger** - macroninja - *http://www.flickr.com/photos/jessekruger/1110294641/* ‖ not oversize...just plus size! - **Brandi Sims** - House Of Sims - *http://www.flickr.com/photos/houseofsims/1061023797* ‖ untitled - **Procsilas Moscas** - procsilas - *http://www.flickr.com/photos/procsilas/11315954* ‖ DSC_1316 - **Daniel danorth1** - *http://www.flickr.com/ photos/danorth1/2310940711* ‖ Sweet Brown Grindage - **Thomas & Dianne Jones** - FreeWine - *http://www.flickr.com/ photos/freewine/307109717*

Purple Photos

Purple top turnips - **Antoaneta** - *http://www.flickr.com/photos/antoaneta/2612913617* ‖ purple shelf and tag - **Anthony Easton** - PinkMoose - *http://www.flickr.com/photos/pinkmoose/550616797* ‖ Glass Curve - **Andreas Levers** - 96dpi - *http://www.flickr.com/photos/96dpi/2921822107* ‖ Tea cups - **gifrancis** - *http://www.flickr.com/photos/ gifrancis/2734874253* ‖ Local color - **Roger H. Goun** - sskennel - *http://www.flickr.com/photos/sskennel/2695594975*

5. Layout

Five Simple Steps - *http://www.fivesimplesteps.co.uk* ‖ White Horse - **Luis Argerich** - *http://www.flickr.com/photos/ lrargerich/3201420582/* ‖ Scout Trooper - **Balakov** - *http://www.flickr.com/photos/balakov/505986437/* ‖ BBC Homepage - *http://www.bbc.co.uk* ‖ Last Supper - *http://en.wikipedia.org/wiki/Last_supper* ‖ Grid Generator - *http:// kematzy.com/blueprint-generator/* ‖ **Drupal iterations** - *drupal.markboultondesign.com/iteration1* ‖ **De Standaard** - *www. standaard.be* ‖ The Future of News by **Oliver Reichenstein**

**Five
Simple
Steps**

A Practical Guide to

Designing
Grid Systems
for the Web

by Mark Boulton

Designing Grid Systems for the Web *by Mark Boulton*

Grid Systems have been used in print design, architecture and interior design for generations. Now, with the advent of the World Wide Web, the same rules of grid system composition and usage no longer apply. Content is viewed in many ways; from RSS feeds, to email. Content is viewed on many devices; from mobile phones to laptops. Users can manipulate the browser, they can remove content, resize the canvas, resize the typefaces. A designer is no longer in control of this presentation.

Designing Grid Systems for the Web is a practical guide to designing visual information structures for the web.

Designing Grid Systems for the Web will be published in **Autumn 2009.**